the BINGE WATCHER'S guide to

BLACK MIRROR

AN UNOFFICIAL COMPANION

Marc W. Polite

The Binge Watcher's Guide to Black Mirror:
An Unofficial Companion © Marc W. Polite 2021

All Rights Reserved. No part of this book may be reproduced or transmitted in any form or by any means, electronic or mechanical, including photocopying, without permission in writing from the publisher.

The Binge Watcher's Guide is a Trademark of Riverdale Avenue Books

For more information contact:
Riverdale Avenue Books
5676 Riverdale Avenue
Riverdale, NY 10471.

www.riverdaleavebooks.com
Design by www.formatting4U.com
Cover by Scott Carpenter

Digital ISBN: 9781626015777
Trade Paperback ISBN: 9781626015784
First Edition, March 2021

Dedication

This book is dedicated to all of the Black Mirror fans out there.

Table of Contents

Introduction 1
The Zeitgeist 7
  What Could Possibly Go Wrong? 8
  Beginnings of Black Mirror 9
  Expanding World of Technology 10
Before You Watch 11
  Season 1: Episodes 1-3 13
  Season 2: Episodes 4-7 33
  Season 3: Episodes 8-13 59
  Season 4: Episodes 14-20 107
  Season 5: Episodes 21-23 163
If You Only Watch One Episode 185
After You've Watched 19191
  Is Black Mirror Anti-Technology? 197
  Future of Black Mirror? 201
  New Twilight Zone Is Not Better Than Black Mirror . 2033
  Dystopia is Now 2055
Appendix 209
About The Author 213

Introduction

In the ongoing pursuit of understanding and describing modern life, there are many sayings that stick in our minds. One such topical saying of unknown origin goes: "May you live in interesting times." In the midst of the 2020 global pandemic many were forced to be home, sheltered in place, and physically distant from one another in efforts to slow down the spread of a deadly virus. And among the things people do with an increased amount of personal time on their hands, is a lot of binge watching. And what more topical choice than Charlie Brooker's *Black Mirror*?

One of the biggest shows on the Netflix streaming platform, *Black Mirror* is fertile ground for multiple discussions about our globally connected society. Named to be a reflection of what it's like to stare at a blank screen—our own face staring back at us—it aims to question the place of technology and social media in our ever-changing world. And in this era of relative social isolation, it is often all you may have to communicate with the outside world.

Created by Charlie Booker and Annabel Jones as an anthology series with a penchant for social commentary on the lasting effects of emerging technology and humanity, *Black Mirror* turns the attention not just towards the tech, but on ourselves. It is one of the most influential, currently active science fiction shows out there, touching on many aspects of the genre and showing us a world that could be. And at the same time, it threatens us with a world not far off.

The technocrats of our era are sure that any emerging technology will be used to solve social problems, but technology does not solve problems—it just develops workarounds. Paradoxically, tech can create new dilemmas… like how much information is too much? Are copies of human consciousness due the same rights as human beings? Should all of our memories and the daily occurrences of our lives be preserved for all time? What does it mean to be sentient? Is there even such a thing as privacy anymore? Much like a shattered screen on a smartphone, we still have to see our broken society and function in it as best as we can. What often happens is that these problems still fester, and technology can work to deepen societal problems like inequality and accentuate issues such as appearance-based discrimination.

Since its debut in 2011, the show has continued to gain popularity. Starting off with just a cult following when it originally aired in the United Kingdom, it has grown to become one of the biggest shows on Netflix and is regarded as the 21st Century version of *The Twilight Zone*.

Brooker, created the series to tell what he terms as "what if" tales—to explore concepts in a short story format. Being a big fan of *The Twilight Zone*, Brooker developed his anthology series at a time where television was embracing five-season story arcs.

Emerging from his affinity for technology, Brooker uses it to tell stories that pull the viewer into a plausible world. The self-contained, singular episode format hasn't been done well in such a long time, but *Black Mirror* was able to pull it off.

As more and more people caught on to the series, *Black Mirror* would also garner recognition. Namely, the show has won numerous awards for its most impactful episodes. In 2018, *Black Mirror* won three Emmy's for the episode "USS Callister," and two Emmy's for "San Junipero." One of these Emmy's was for "Outstanding Television Movie," an indication of how well the show was received in the United States. *Black Mirror* would also win awards from BAFTA (British Academy of Film and Television Arts), the Art Directors Guild, and an award from AMPS (Association of Motion Picture Sound) In total, according to IMDB, *Black Mirror* has an impressive total of 32 wins and 93 nominations.

Much like the original *Twilight Zone*, *Black Mirror* has a legion of fans that have yet to have been christened with a nickname. Dr. Who fans are called Whovians, Star Trek fans are called Trekkies or Trekkers, and *Black Mirror* fans are called paranoid.

In this compendium, we will be discussing all five seasons of *Black Mirror*, as well as the interactive movie *Bandersnatch*. There is a lot here to discuss, and I know that we are all looking forward to getting into it. If you start with the very first episode, it might weird you out. But, it doesn't represent the entire series—there is so much more to it than that. While it doesn't matter which episode you start with, I do recommend any other than the first.

Marc W. Polite

This is a project for fans, by a fan, but not for fans only. It is also for those who want to get into *Black Mirror*. This is a book for those who want to understand what all the hype is about. Welcome to *The Binge Watchers Guide to Black Mirror!*

WARNING

There are spoilers in every part of this book after this introduction. Should you continue, be forewarned. Okay, there's my disclaimer. Let's go!

The Zeitgeist

Black Mirror has been influential, and eerily predictive as well. Whether it be the abuses of big data, a political scandal, or invasions of privacy, this anthology series stretches far and wide when it comes to what it assesses as the post-modern human condition. Constantly, unabashedly, it goes to dark places, using our social relations to show us who we truly are. Despite the instant contact that we often have with one another, *Black Mirror* highlights the ironic disconnection that comes with it.

And that says nothing for how predictive it is. Some episodes in their content predicted an election, and what tech would emerge later in the decade of the 2010's. This series has been prescient and made a number of spot on calls as to how we would be living in the not so distant future. The angst that some of us feel about the potential applications of technology are often times justified, as we see over five seasons.

We live in the age of digital media, where information is available instantaneously. And *Black Mirror* captures these potential unforeseen consequences of new tech so accurately that it has become shorthand for how wrong things can go.

Marc W. Polite

What Could Possibly Go Wrong?

There is a concept in social science called the law of unintended consequences. While not as ironclad as natural law, this concept does have some usage in pointing out what can happen that wasn't necessarily foreseeable. Let's look at one current, real world example for a moment just to get an idea of the notion.

In online news, the bigger, more established outlets can put limitations on the availability of their content. If you visit a site, you may be allowed to view no more than 10 articles freely within a month's time. Your information access is restricted behind what is known as a paywall—the mechanism that the publisher is using to fund their publication and maintain a revenue stream. If you do not subscribe to the news site, you won't be able to see any additional content.

Paying for access to the site of a news publication can be cost prohibitive for many people. Because of this, what is left are sites that aren't behind a paywall. But these may not be as trustworthy or rigorous in vetting information as established sources. Unfortunately, these sites—and those like them—can proliferate, and are often amplified on social media sites. It is a case in point that typifies the old adage about a lie traveling around the world, and the truth hasn't even stepped out of the house. Instead of being a safeguard for the funding of credible journalism, the paywall is one of many things that fueled the proliferation of disinformation.

The stated intention was to promote the funding of news, but the resulting paradox is that many more sources are questionable. Just something to think about when your next phone notification goes off with Breaking News. If current technology has unintended consequences, then they will definitely exist in newer innovations.

Beginnings of Black Mirror

Black Mirror is not the first project Charlie Brooker has ever done. Previously, Brooker did a show on BBC Four called *Screenwipe* that lasted from 2006 to 2008. *Screenwipe* was a show Brooker used to review and comment on various British television shows. One wouldn't know it from *Black Mirror*, but Charlie Brooker can be quite a comedic writer.

Brooker cites *Twilight Zone* as one of his influences, and sought to create an anthology series that was poignant and contemporary. At the time of its creation, science fiction TV programming was in somewhat of a lull. The last science fiction show with a big fan base, *Battlestar Galactica*, had been off the air for three years. In 2011, it was all about shows like *Game of Thrones*, and *The Walking Dead*, while what fans call "hard science fiction" took a back seat on television. These shows had their fan bases of course, but there was a void for fans that gravitated towards topical science and the technology in them.

In 2011, the political world was in turmoil with the Arab Spring, and the populist outburst of Occupy Wall Street here in the United States. The former was even mentioned in the very first episode "The National Anthem." *Black Mirror* debuted with little fanfare towards the end of the year on Channel 4, a British television station. The first two seasons stayed on this channel, not hitting Netflix until December of 2014—three years later.

Marc W. Polite

Expanding World of Technology

According to *Scientific American*, the human brain has the capacity of 2.5 petabytes (a petabyte is a million gigabytes.) It is entirely possible that in the next few decades, technology will have the capacity to back up an entire human brain on a hard drive. While we hope this doesn't result in an Arnim Zola from *Captain America: Winter Soldier*, it is intriguing.

In reflecting on the last decade of technology, we have seen the distribution of ideas through mostly web-based tech. This proliferation of streamed content, and telepresence software, has meant a noted change in collaborative projects. Lag and snafus aside, these systems are a lot more advanced than they were ten years ago. And, given the reality of Moore's Law, they are sure to get more sophisticated as time passes.

Before You Watch

Before you begin watching *Black Mirror*, be sure to cast all of your science fiction stereotypes to the side. This show is not about aliens, plane-sized weapons, or epic space battles. Don't worry yourself about learning about wormholes, faster than light travel, or futuristic techno-babble. The science here is probable—a projection into the future grounded in what exists now. The stories are more about the characters, and how they cope in a world not too far from today.

In a time where computing power and the access to it becomes ubiquitous, the battles are fought with each person deciding how to use this technology. Also, take care to notice that there will be episodes that are plausible to occur right here, and right now.

With the exception of Season 4, every season of *Black Mirror* has an episode that could technically happen today, with existing technology. It constantly blurs the line between contemporary commentary and science fiction, making you think hard about how our usage of technology is already too far gone for us to put the worms back in the can, so to speak.

Also, a big part of understanding and truly appreciating *Black Mirror*, is noticing the connections between episodes. While the show is in an anthology format with self-contained stories and no sequential episodes, there are frequent references to past episodes in later seasons. You can think of it as a shared universe, so to speak. Across seasons, there will be songs that you can't get out of your head, as well as multiple Easter eggs.

These connections make this series more interesting, and give an idea of how adjacent these developments are. At this point, there are no recurring characters, but do watch for some actors to make additional appearances in different roles.

Another thing that would help is to understand the concept of cloud storage. To give you a quick idea of what cloud storage is, it is pretty much when you store information on a computer server in a remote location. As opposed to merely saving data on a hard drive or a thumb drive, cloud storage is an alternative way to have backups of vital information. Examples of cloud storage available for personal usage are services like DropBox and OneDrive. There can be security issues of course, but it is convenient to use. Not that you have to be super technical, but the term will come up in more than a few episodes.

Season 1

Episode 1: The National Anthem

Aired: December 4, 2011
Director: Otto Bathurst
Writer: Charlie Brooker
Cast: Rory Kinnear (Michael Callow), Lindsay Duncan (Alex Cairns), Donald Sumpter (Julian Hereford), Tom Goodman Hill (Tom Blice), Anna Wilson Jones (Jane Callow), Patrick Kennedy (Section Chief Walker), Alastair Mckenzie (Martin), Chetna Pandya (Malaika), Alex Macqueen (Special Agent Callett), Jay Simpson (Flynn/Rod Senseless), Lydia Wilson (Princess Susannah)

"The World's Bloody Broken!"

The very first episode of this science fiction anthology series is not very high tech at all. As such, it is also the must realistic. Here, the prime minister Michael Callow finds himself to be the subject of blackmail. Terrorists have kidnapped Princess Susannah, threatening to kill her unless Callow has intercourse with a pig on live television.

What a way to open a series, huh? Equal parts spectacle, dark humor, and voyeurism, *The National Anthem* is a punch in the throat for a series about the possible abuses of technology. This is an episode that is jarring not only because of the subject matter, but because it is also plausible it could occur right now.

Prime Minister Callow finds himself at the whim of technologically savvy foes with a penchant for making statements. His team of advisors are completely out of sorts, unable to deal with what is unfolding right in front of them. As the episode carries on, we see the mainstream media play second fiddle to social media. Just as we see in our reality, social media moves at a rate much faster than news organizations are able to, and can get the word out in short moments.

As we see Callow's team falter, it depicts the breakdown and failure of the official response. The viewer, in a tragicomic fashion, sees his handlers go from trying to fool the cyber-terrorists with visual trickery, to bringing in the military to apprehend the suspect. But as both of these attempts fail, the realization sets in that Callow has to go through with the demands. He and his team have screwed the pooch, so to speak.

We also see how quickly public opinion can turn on a person in the public eye. Callow was initially regarded as a tragic figure stuck between two hard decisions, but after multiple failed attempts to apprehend the kidnappers, he was seen only as selfish. It became necessary then, for the prime minister to do what he needed to in order to save Princess Susanna's life.

The prime minister commits the act… and we are forced to half-watch—a reminder of internet voyeur culture, guided by the principle of what has been seen can't be unseen. However, unbeknownst to Callow, Princess Susanna is released unharmed, half an hour before the stated deadline for him to complete the lewd act.

The kidnapper also kills himself, to escape apprehension. There is no lesson here, no big moral to the story, just a kidnapper who held a public figure hostage just because they could. Talk about nihilism. This is a theme that will be revisited more than a few times. This episode just raises so many questions about our society. One of which is, what can you compel someone to do in a life or death situation?

This is the world we find ourselves in—one where public humiliation is at the ready, and people can have you on the hook for very little. As we all know, but collectively push to the back of our minds, all of our information is out there ready for use or misuse. This is a theme that will be explored in a later episode, but for now just note how easy it is to set up a political figure using current technology.

Considering that social media is such a spectacle, public humiliation is always an option for the targeted. It may not be as extreme as blackmail, but the potential for ongoing abuse is ever present; it's incredibly difficult to suppress information once it is already out there. In a world where social media moves faster than news organizations, and what is trending on Twitter can determine the focus of the news, public opinion becomes a fickle, transient thing that can shift at a moment's notice.

In a way, this is a predicament where we are all held hostage.

Held hostage to past tweets, old status updates, and beliefs that an individual may have evolved out of—this is our post-modern society. Individuals are held accountable, while institutions are not. And there's no unknowing once we know the depths of depravity apparent in our modern culture. Like a member of Callow's cabinet says, "there is no playbook" for this at all. In a sense, the realization sets in that we're all screwed.

Episode 2: Fifteen Million Merits

Aired: December 11, 2011
Director: Euros Lyn
Writer: Charlie Brooker, Konnie Huq
Cast: Daniel Kaluuya (Bingham Madsen), Jessica Brown Findlay (Abi Khan), Rupert Everett (Judge Hope), Julia Davis (Judge Charity), Ashley Thomas (Judge Wraith), Paul Popplewell (Dustin), Isabella Laughland (Swift), Hannah John-Kamen (Selma Telse),

> *"You don't see people up here, it's all fodder."*
> *–Bing Madsen*

How badly do you want to make it? Are you willing to compromise everything you believe in to improve your life? This is the question that confronts Bingham Madsen in *Fifteen Million Merits*. Imagine a near future society, where there are no more fossil fuels and everyone has to create electricity. One where you are obligated to peddle on an electricity-generating bicycle to secure a digital currency that you need to buy toothpaste or even wash your hands.

Bing wakes up in a very small living quarters, surrounded by four walls made of screens. The screens show a digital farm, complete with a digital rooster functioning as his alarm clock. In addition to this, ads can pop up on the screen at almost any moment, much like the internet today. The key difference in this society however, is that there are financial penalties incurred for skipping these ads, or even muting the audio. If you shut your eyes, the screens prompt you to resume viewing. Talk about a captive audience!

To make matters worse, there is a strict hierarchy in this episode that's based on fitness. If you are deemed too big to produce electricity on a bike, you will be reassigned as a cleaner of the workplace. There is open fat shaming and body positivity is non-existent. We see one of Bing's co-workers struggling to keep up on the bike, while the office jack-hole jokes that he will soon be wearing the lemon suit—the uniform cleaners wear as they tidy up. Devalued as human beings, they are shown as examples of what not to allow yourself to become. Even though their work is essential for the continued function of the society, they are still looked down upon. Sounds kind of familiar, doesn't it?

"Fifteen Million Merits" depicts a society of screens and micro-transactions. It depicts a future where, much like today, society is obsessed with productivity. We see there are even leader boards that show who is the leading peddler in the office. Bing is one of many people in this facility who is resigned to the way things are. He looks simply bored with the drudgery, much like many working people are with their normal jobs. Bing is so tuned out, that he doesn't notice that there is a woman quietly admiring him.

That is until a new employee, Abi, joins his section. Bing is noticeably interested in Abi, and interacts with her awkwardly at first. But as he gradually gets to know her, he opens up about his past. He tells her that his brother passed away last year, and while he received inherited merits, he doesn't quite know what to do with them. He just doesn't see the value in buying pointless avatars and intangibles.

Eventually, Bing hears Abi singing in the unisex bathroom. The song in question, "Anyone Who Knows What Love Is" by Irma Thomas, has become most associated with *Black Mirror*. If you listen carefully, you'll hear it in every season. This leads to one afternoon, while on a meal break, where he finds the words he needs to say.

Complimenting Abi on her singing voice, Bing suggests that she audition for the talent show *Hot Shots*, the episode's futuristic version of *American Idol*. However, there is a price to auditioning—one that Bing offers to, quite literally, pay. Gifting Abi the 15 million merits to audition, he manages to talk her into going on the show.

He goes with her to the audition, where she impresses both the judges and the digital audience. This is a budding story of a love interest doing a favor for a person, only to have it go left. To his horror, Bing witnesses as the three hosts redirect her aspirations as a singer into pressure to become a porn star.

In this audition, we see a few methods of coercion at play. Foremost, we see appearance-based discrimination that confronts anyone who wants to go into the entertainment industry. Further, the comments of Judge Wraith are clearly sexual harassment and a representation of what aspiring female artists have to deal with.

Judge Charity on another hand, says that there are

already enough singers slotted in on her stream. Supposedly the voice of reason, Judge Charity reminds Abi that she either takes the deal from Wraith, or its back on the bike for her. They remind her that others would give anything to be in her position, thus magnifying the pressure. The three hosts do a combination of cajoling and berating her, bullying Abi into taking the degrading out. The digital audience even gets in on the pressure, chanting to do it repeatedly. Wanting to escape the routine of the bicycle, and influenced by a drugged drink given to her before the audition, Abi hesitantly agrees.

Beside himself, Bing was removed from the audition by studio security. He is crushed. We see him depressed about the outcome, eating lunch in the cafeteria by himself and lamenting over what was destroyed by what he could not have foreseen. The only memento that he had was an origami penguin Abi made for him as a token of her appreciation. He would remain in this dejected state until he went home that night, only to be forced to witness her erotic debut.

In what would become typical *Black Mirror* fashion, Bing is unable to skip this stream, due to a lack of merits after having drained his account to pay for Abi's audition. He tries to turn around, but the screen pans to the wall that he's facing. There is no escape from this, try as he might. Even closing his eyes is met by a high-pitched alarm in his domicile, accompanied by a "resume viewing" prompt on the screen. Further, the digital handle to his room would not open during the commercial. He has no choice, but to witness the woman he has feelings for get ran through on a live stream.

This is what makes him lose it.

Bing slams into the walls of the screen, throws his mattress at it, and pounds with his fists until a shard of glass drops from it. Considering his state of mind, it looks as if he might take it and end his life right then and there. And yet, he has bigger plans.

Not typified as the most dedicated employee, Bing began to show up earlier to work to get more peddling in. He spends as little merits as he can, choosing to eat the food that other employees waste. We see him practicing a dance routine in his living quarters, in preparation. It's obvious that he is grinding out enough merits to buy himself a ticket to audition on *Hot Shots*.

And within two months, he accomplishes what normally takes people six, and purchases a golden ticket. When he enters the *Hot Shots* audition area, he takes with him the empty box of Cuppliance that Abi had drank. He shows it to the backstage producer, fooling her into thinking that he had the stuff already.

After introducing himself as an entertainer, he begins his dance routine. Part of the way through it however, he pulls out the shard of glass hidden in his waistband and holds it to his throat. He threatens to slice his own throat if security tries to remove him before he says his piece to the audience.

And once Bing speaks, he has a rant for the ages. This was one of the most memorable rants I've heard since Howard Beale's "I'm Mad as Hell, and I'm Not going to Take It Anymore" creed in the 1976 movie *Network*. Bing criticizes not only the panel of judges, but the entire society. There's no way to do it justice in just a recap—you have to see it for yourself. It goes over really well with the audience, despite its abrasive nature.

Arguably, this is the appearance that made Daniel Kaluuya a star, as he would go on to do *Get Out* and *Black Panther*.

Unfazed, however, Judge Hope says that he would like to hear him talk again, offering him a slot on his stream twice a week. And as Bing accepts—even without the influence of the Cuppliance—the same panel that sent Abi into a life of porn sends him into one of social commentary. One propped up by the very society he claims to criticize.

In the next scene, his old co-workers are flipping through different streams that they are watching while they peddle at work and come across Bing's broadcast. Here, Bing is giving a much less passionate commentary, while still holding the shard of glass to his neck. That same shard of glass has now also become an avatar item that those watching can purchase.

As the stream ends, the camera pans out to show Bing living in a much bigger apartment. There's a penguin on his desk—a nod to the origami one Abi had given him. In the last shot, we see him holding a glass of orange juice, looking out at images of a forest on a broader set of screens.

The ending of "Fifteen Million Merits" is the outcome of pitting an individual against society. Despite Bing's strong will, and his outrage at the living conditions that everyone must deal with, he takes the first opportunity to get out of his own drudgery. The future is a world of spectators, not participants. So why not parlay what he said to improve his individual predicament? It's a choice that many people would have taken, even if Bing will now have to dilute and section out his message so that he can have material for his show.

That's the reality of institutions, social norms, and their ability to mold human behavior. Bing's message of truth against the existing power structure is now incorporated into that very system, expressed on a live stream. It's an example of what political scientists call controlled opposition. Given a platform to voice the frustration of the masses, the very people responsible and complicit in this oppression are able to control the narrative. If you control the platform, you can determine how far their message will go in condemning things as they are. And by turning it into a commodity, you downplay the severity of it.

This episode represents the issue of co-optation of radical voices and the shortcomings of a single voice movement. When we look at American history, we see so many times when the message of a movement starts off radical, but is gradually watered down and comercialized to make it palatable to a wider audience. You can start out marching around the community with raised fists and black battle fatigues, yet end up on the cover of magazines with a myriad of paid panel discussions. The machine can take your rage and use you to dole it out it small doses.

The truth is for sale, and your truth is there to be monetized.

His rant, while passionate, didn't change anything socially. The messenger is bought off and the system continues on as it was. Their extremely punitive world with rigid social rules carries on, without missing a beat. The realistic depiction of the prison like nature of social class, is that the brutal nature of it robs people of their voices, and changes your tune if you speak out.

The bottom line is that people don't change institutions—institutions change people. And it's captured really well in "Fifteen Million Merits." At first, we see the bikes and could think that he was at the gym. But we quickly see the compulsory nature of it, the devaluing of those who are unsuitable to meet the demands of this society. It forces people to peddle endlessly while promoting classism and valuing people solely based upon their looks. What is this, but a more refined and honest version of what we have now? With fat shaming weaponized as a marker of a person's lack of productivity, it takes away the pretext of many who carry these attitudes under the guise of concern. For those who are driven to desperation, an out is provided, but it will cost you your dignity. Finally, for those who take issue with the entirety of the situation, you are given a safe perch to launch your tirades.

While Bing is critical of the whole society, he takes the first out he was offered to improve his station in life. But there is no shame in that—it's what the majority of us would do if provided the chance. Is that not what the idea of social mobility is all about? To borrow a term from another science fiction mainstay, *The Matrix*, Bing decides to take the blue pill. No point in going back to the same drudgery if it is possible to do better.

In a future society that cultivates public ridicule and shame, the joke is on anyone who thinks that it will change from just speaking out. This is why the commodification of a message occurs. Even dissent can be molded into something that is not a threat to the existing order. Blowing off steam is not changing or challenging anything, it's just adding to yet another of the pre-assigned filters.

Being an activist against the society in which you live can be a demoralizing experience. You can, at times, feel that the mightiest of efforts can all be undone with such ease. It can lead to a sense of futility and is why so many people acquiesce to their surroundings, no matter how much they may not like it. It goes to show how easy it is to co-opt even the most strident voices for reform, as one individual cannot truly stand against the power of those in charge alone.

Episode 3: The Entire History of You

Aired: December 18, 2011
Director: Brian Welsh
Writer: Jesse Armstrong
Cast: Toby Kebbell (As Liam Foxwell), Jodie Whitaker (Ffion Foxwell), Tom Cullen (Jonas), Jimi Mistry (Paul), Amy Beth Hayes (Lucy), Rebekah Staton (Colleen)

"Not everything that isn't true, is a lie, Liam"
–Ffion Foxwell

How far would you go to confirm a suspicion? What if you could probe your own memories, and the memories of those around you for clues? Are you sure you really want to find the answers you're looking for? These are questions that Liam Foxwell faces in "The Entire History of You."

Liam is a struggling lawyer, married, and the father of a young child. It's a future where an implant behind your ear, called the Grain, records your daily occurrences in full video and audio. You can even playback your recordings on a screen, similar to casting a streaming service today. Sounds cool, doesn't it?

During a dinner gathering, he and his wife Ffion

speak with an old friend who no longer has their grain device. Much like not having a social media today, to go without a grain is seen as counter-culture. So ingrained is this technology that even their child has the device implanted. They watch their daughter's "re-do" to ensure that the babysitter was doing what they were supposed to. No need for a nanny camera here, huh?

What Liam is not initially aware of is that his wife has been intimately involved with another one of their guests, Jonas. The episode follows Liam as he spirals into his memories, using the grain to pick up on things that only raise his suspicions. He catches how talkative she was with Jonas and contrasts it to how clammed up she was beside him at the table. He notices how Ffion laughs at something that Jonas said that wasn't all that funny.

Liam runs everything back, obsessing over subtle differences in his wife's behavior and body language. Imagine running back conversations in your mind, accurately word for word. And imagine being able to confront people with it. That would be akin to mining for metadata on interpersonal relationships, and goes far beyond what we have access to today.

Turns out, Ffion and Jonas had had a fling back in college. It was one of those situations that Ffion once downplayed, but now it has resurfaced. Jonas, the guy she told Liam not to worry about, is a nagging discomfort for him now. After a slight argument over her past history, the two have make-up sex, but both are watching past footage in their grains. We have no way of knowing if this was "re-dos" of their past encounters, or with other people. Kind of a higher tech

The Binge Watcher's Guide to Black Mirror

version of being with someone, but thinking of somebody else during the act.

Later, Liam confronts Jonas in a drunken rage. Going as far as his home, he threatens him and demanding that he delete the old footage his college times with his wife. Using a broken wine bottle, Liam forces Jonas to wipe the recordings, under threat of getting his implant gouged out. Jonas complies, and watches Liam as he drunkenly stumbles back to his car.

Confronting Ffion, Liam discovers that Jonas slept with his wife 18 months ago while they weren't on speaking terms. The most hurtful part however, is Liam's realization that his daughter Jodie may not be his. While never confirmed on screen, it's hard to blame him for his mind going down that road—and further, driving him over the edge.

Now alone in an empty house and feeling his whole life fall apart around him, Liam wallows in the past, playing back memories of happier times with Ffion and his daughter. The episode ends with him taking a razor blade to himself, slicing the area just behind his ear, and pulling the grain device out. The screen goes dark, reminiscent of Oedipus, who gouged out his own eyes upon learning the truth. It's a tragic outcome, leaving Liam a victim of his paranoia and suspicion, aided and abetted by technology. He didn't have it in him to just leave it alone, needing to know exactly what happened.

There's no moral here, not really—just the possible reality of knowing too much. Should Liam have kept prying, at the risk of breaking his own heart? Or should he have just let things be and gone through the motions to keep his family together? There's no easy answer, and what we know about other people doesn't make it easier. In this era of digital forensics, where people can go through text messages and such for evidence of infidelity, this episode hits hard.

In our modern world, your entire life is under a microscope, which also means that your relationships with others are also subject to scrutiny. With social media, things rather forgotten are easily dredged back up. Most users, for instance, have had the experience of a Facebook memory popping up from years ago, with pictures of you and others that you don't deal with anymore. Whether it was a friendship, or a romance, you see it, wince a little bit, and refresh the timeline. Our lives are already on rewind in a sense—this episode merely a vision of what the future might bring.

Fun Fact: Jodie Whitaker would go on to be the new Doctor in *Doctor Who*, another big science fiction show.

Season 2

Episode 1: Be Right Back

Aired: February 11, 2013
Director: Owen Harris
Writer: Charlie Brooker
Cast: Hayley Atwell (As Martha Powell), Domhnall Gleeson (Ash Starmer), Claire Keelan (Naomi), Sinead Matthews (Sarah), Flora Nicholson (Midwife), Glenn Hanning (Delivery Man), Tim Delap (Simon), Indira Ainger (Martha's Daughter)

> *"It's a thief, that thing."*
> –Martha Powell (pointing to Ash's phone)

Death may not be final in the future. With many of our interactions being documented on social media, the notion of a digital afterlife is very much an ethereal concept. But what would that look like? How would we react to such a thing? This is something that Martha Powell comes to confront in "Be Right Back."

Martha and Ash are a married couple who have been together for 10 years. Ash, like many people nowadays, spends most of his time on his phone and social media. Early on we catch him thumbing through his timeline, only half hearing Martha ask a question. His attention here isn't what's necessarily important, but rather his connection with his device.

Because after he passes away in a car crash, it's that digital footprint that's left of him.

But his funeral would not be the end of this story—rather just the eerie beginning. At Ash's funeral, Martha's friend Sarah tells her about a service that would let her communicate with her now deceased husband. Compiling emails, texts, tweets, and status updates, the service folds them all into a schematic that results in a facsimile of ones social media presence. Able to mimic what the person would say given any scenario, it's practically the beginning of automation for human life.

Initially, Martha finds the idea revolting and tells Sarah that she wants nothing to do with it. She sees it as obscene, perverse, and ultimately disrespectful to the memory of Ash. And yet, despite her objections, Sara still signs her up for a trial run. What a good friend.

And when she inevitably gets an email from Ash, things start to get weird.

Martha is hesitant to answer the program mimicking her deceased husband, but soon finds herself chatting back and forth with "Ash." Adding to the awkwardness of it all, Martha is pregnant and never had the chance to tell him. And so she tells the program instead. As time goes on, it learns more and more about their relationship and, eventually, is able to verbally talk to Martha—an additional service that the once skeptic eagerly accepts.

Prompted by "Ash," Martha gives the service permission to compile all of Ash's social media pages, emails, voice recordings, and text messages to combine into one program that would communicate just like him. Not informal emails, actual conversation. But that's not the end of it. "Ash" informs Martha that there is yet another level to the service.

For all intents and purposes, the program at this point is the remains of Ash's mind. The only difference Martha can spot between the two of them is the lack of a body. So naturally, that's exactly what she orders. Enter the body double of Ash, an android made up of synthetic flesh. Using pictures and video of the departed, it's able to become a doppelganger of that person. Sitting the android in the bathtub, Martha gives it a few hours for the "mind" of Ash to sync from the cloud and into the new body.

Now imagine your dead husband came walking downstairs to greet you. How would you react? How would that even feel? That's where the real meat of the episode is.

Martha tries her best to adjust to the doppelganger of her late husband, including of course trying to teach it how to be intimate with her. And she can't hide the intrigue on her face when it tells her that it can turn its erection on and off at will. Unlike the real Ash who had a "lasting" issue however, the android has no such limitations and is able to go as long as Martha could ever want. Further, it was able to learn what she liked on the fly thanks to having the entire internet at its disposal. Apparently the new Ash knew the directions to "pound town."

However, despite all of the adjustment there was still one major issue—machines can't do nuance. The thing is, all the aspects of a person's personality cannot simply be captured by a program. Martha begins to see this as her new Ash behaves just like an automaton, doing exactly as she says with no push back. After all, she is the *administrator* of the android, not its partner.

Sure, the doppelganger looks like a younger version of Ash having adjusted its features to look like more flattering pictures of him. But it lacked his nuances, his personality, what he was like in life. You can't even say that new Ash was emotionally unavailable, because synthetic humans can't have true emotions. The original may have been constantly checked out on his phone, but he was still there in a sense.

After an argument and tired of struggling with an imitation who is not the person she loved, Martha exclaims, "you're not enough of him" and kicks him out of the house. Not permitted to go more than 25 meters away from where he was activated, this new Ash resigns to standing outside like a simple lawn gnome.

Martha follows it outside, taking it as far as a nearby cliff and debates telling it to jump. But after arguing with the doppelganger about how Ash wouldn't have just done everything she wanted, she realizes that she's not capable of going through with it. Killing the doppelganger would be like losing him all over again. She screams out into the void, feeling completely defeated, and ultimately takes it back home.

The story ends with a flash forward to her daughter bringing her "dad" a slice of birthday cake in the attic. Tucked away like something she wishes she could forget, the new Ash lives isolated in the attic of the house, with all of the other unwanted clutter. A very odd ending.

If you'll bear with me, let's do a little bit of comparative science fiction. The concept of restoring

The Binge Watcher's Guide to Black Mirror

entire beings has been done before in *Battlestar Galactica*. The Resurrection Hubs—the ships where the Cylon's coding and programming "essence" return to a new body after being destroyed—are one example. In the short lived BSG spin off *Caprica*, we get an explanation of this technology from Zoey Graystone, daughter of the creator of the first Cybernetic Life Node:

"The human brain contains roughly 300 megabytes of information. Not much when you get right down to it. The question isn't how to store it, it's how to access it. You can't download a personality. There's no way to translate the data. But the information being held in our heads is available in other databases. People leave more than footprints as they travel through life... medical scans, DNA profiles, psych evaluations, school records, emails, recording, video, audio, cat scans genetic typing, synaptic records, security cameras, test results, shopping records, talent shows, ball games, traffic tickets, restaurant bills, phone records, music lists, movie tickets, TV shows... even prescriptions for birth control."

These are all part of everyone's digital footprint, and them outliving us is our emerging reality. Instead of grieving, and acknowledging the loss, "Be Right Back" creates a Catch-22 where Martha is both allowed to move on, and not, at the same time.

Worth noting is that this story is the first time *Black Mirror* deals with death and loss. There are a lot of themes here about grief, and healing, and it's arguable that Martha never really gave herself a chance to grieve, because she was signed up for the program against her will. In a sense, the new Ash prolonged her grieving process indefinitely. When she first dropped the phone, she freaked out similar to losing him again. During the second level of restoration, we saw the awkwardness of Martha trying to teach a programmable body double to be more like a human being.

The doppelganger did not know, nor have a way of processing, how it sleeping with its eyes open would make her uncomfortable. It did not know how to pretend to breathe or understand why it should do that. A program that was meant to ease the grieving process, only ended up making it worse. It made Martha miss Ash even more, because there is more to a human being than a body and composite of publicly posted content.

Have you ever had a Facebook friend that passed away? You acknowledge that they are gone, but you don't delete them as a friend. You know that they will not see it, but when their birthday comes up, you acknowledge it with a comment on their timeline. This has become our modern way of paying tribute to the memory of the person. But the reality is we won't always have access to the people around us, so we might want to give pause and think about how much they mean to us when it comes to the here and now.

In life, Ash was like so many people in this era—attached to his phone. And it ended up stealing time from him and Martha's relationship. When she loses him, all she has left is his child, and his digital footprint on social media. And of course, an unfeeling machine that can never stop reminding her of what, exactly, it was that she lost.

Episode 2: White Bear

Aired: February 18, 2013
Director: Carl Tibbetts
Writer: Charlie Brooker
Cast: Lenora Crichlow (As Victoria Skillane), Michael Smiley (Baxter), Tuppence Middleton (Jem), Ian Bonar (Damien), Nick Ofield (Ian Rannoch), Russell Barnett (Reporter), Imani Jackman (Jemima Sykes)

"Where the fuck have you been?!" –Jem

In the near future, we will have a number of ways to punish people. But, the age-old question of whether or not the punishment fits the crime will still remain relevant. Something Victoria Skillane will have to come to terms with in the terrifying "White Bear" episode.

In what can be considered a cross between *The Truman Show* and *The Purge*, we are introduced to a person who doesn't remember who she is, having to avoid strangers that are trying to kill her—she doesn't know why. Worse, people all over are watching and filming with their smartphones.

The episode begins with Victoria waking up with a massive headache, a bottle of pills spilled on the floor in front of her. She's in a house that is unfamiliar to her, with every screen displaying a mysterious white symbol. She sees a picture of a young girl, and picks it up thinking that it might be her daughter. When she does, however, her sight glitches causing another headache. Outside, a bunch of people are filming. And just as she goes out, a man with the white block symbol pulls up, pulls out a shotgun, and starts chasing after her.

Victoria runs, calling out in vain for the strangers filming her to help. That is until she meets Jem who, alongside her companion Damien, smuggles her into a nearby convenience store. She manages to help Victoria escape the man, but not before he kills Damien.

Jem explains to her that some kind of signal appeared on every television, turning most people into what they call watchers. And those unaffected became hunters, doing whatever they wanted, including killing others. At one point when Victoria almost looks at one of the phones, Jem freaks out exclaiming "Don't Look At It!" She pulls out a taser and tells her that the signal is coming from the phones.

The crowd of hunters eventually catches up with them, but they are rescued by a man named Baxter. As he drives them into the safety of the woods, Victoria starts to remember, but her memories are still too foggy to make out. Then, without warning—and to the surprise of no one—Baxter pulls out a shotgun and marches the two of them off into the trees. He's going to torture Victoria and let people watch.

Jem manages to escape when Baxter takes a phone call, leaving Victoria alone with dead people strung up on trees. Frustrated that one got away, he takes out a power drill with the intention of using it on Victoria. But before he is able to do any damage, Jem returns with the shotgun and shoots him in the back. From there, Jem takes Baxter's keys, and drives Victoria to the TV station with the intent to burn it down, interrupting the signal that is affecting everyone.

At the TV station they are met by another two hunters, one of whom manages to stabs Jem. Victoria manages to wrestle the shotgun from the other, firing it into his chest, but he's unharmed. Not because he's invincible, but rather because when she fires, confetti comes out. Two doors suddenly open up behind her, revealing a cheering audience. And we realize that this was all a show. Victoria just wasn't aware of it.

The watchers and hunters all come out onto the stage, restraining Victoria into a chair by her wrists and ankles. The producer then appears, proceeding to tell her exactly who she is.

A video is played on giant monitors showing how she and her fiancé kidnapped Jemima Sykes—the girl in the photo from earlier—took her to a forest, and killed her. Victoria did nothing to stop him, choosing to capture the entire ordeal on her smartphone. We see that the reoccurring symbol that she had been seeing was representative of a white teddy bear—one of Jemima's possessions that was found in the forest. It since became a symbol of pursuit for justice. While her fiancé avoided final sentencing by committing suicide in prison, the country wanted to ensure that the same thing would not happen with Victoria.

The whole episode, we were led to believe that she was the victim. We were sympathetic to Victoria, until we find out what she did. The reality is that she was an accessory to the murder of an innocent child and the ongoing punishment, was for her to relive each day being hunted anew. And at the end of each day, a neural device is placed on her head and erases the last 24 hours, so she can relive the horror fresh, and the show can go on.

"White Bear" is a story about crime and punishment. And we have no idea how long Victoria is slated to endure her torture. The White Bear Justice Park—the reality of this world—is a way of monetizing the suffering of Victoria Skellane, giving park attendees a chance to participate in her punishment. While some of the people she encounters day to day are paid actors, the men and women filming her on their phones are all park guests.

Victoria understandably begs to die. Some could say this is a futuristic version of cruel and unusual punishment, but that depends on your perspective. Considering that this episode is set in Britain—which does not have a death penalty—some might say this is fair game. They might also say that to just kill her would be barbaric. And it can be left up to the audience to decide what, exactly, is too much.

"White Bear" is an individualized horror story that places Victoria in her own living hell. Throughout the episode, she is given false hope after false hope, only to relive it again and again, day after day. One can draw parallels to the ancient myth of Sisyphus, who is sentenced to forever roll a giant boulder up a hill in Hades. The boulder always dislodges, rolling back down and wasting all of his efforts. Victoria, in a similar vein, is made to believe that she can change the world, perhaps even save it, but is never able to.

This setting of an unattainable, impossible task is a concept in eternal punishment, and it is explored here to horrifying effect. Being denied the memory of your experiences is especially cruel. What do you have, if anything, without your memories? Not only does it prolong her suffering, it can never allow her to emotionally atone for her crime.

Further, "White Bear" explores the way the bystander effect weighs on the person who needs help. There are segments of our society that just seem to thrive on watching things happen, without doing anything to intervene. Think of rubber necking in traffic. In reality shows, we watch the lives of celebrities and highlight all their triumphs and failures. We watch the social media timelines of people rather than having conversations with them. We even watch people fight in the street, and—like in the episode—see people just pulling out their phones, filming and laughing in the background.

We are even subject to watching people die on camera, as the footage of how it happens circulates across social media. Some say that people eventually become desensitized to that sort of thing, but it is far from the truth. There are deleterious effects on the psyches of people, even those who witness second hand trauma. Collective passivity is cultivated, and it has led to a society where we just watch events transpire. People are incentivized not to intervene, as doing so can put them at risk as well.

Of course, the bystander effect predates social media. But it certainly doesn't make it any better. With that being said, these platforms do present chances to see what is wrong with our society. So, why not monetize it for all to see? Why not use what is already prevalent and re-purpose it? At the end of "White Bear," we are shocked. But why? Is this individualized horror story a bit too punitive? Maybe. But then you just shrug your shoulders, and you go on to the next episode. Worse things happen in real life.

This is the first time the white bear symbol would be featured in a *Black Mirror* episode. But, it will not be the last. Much like the choices and consequences of Victoria Skillane's actions, this symbol will become one of different paths and possibilities. So keep an eye out.

Episode 3: The Waldo Moment

Aired: February 25th, 2013
Director: Bryn Higgins
Writer: Charlie Brooker
Cast: Daniel Rigby (As Jamie Salter), Chloe Pirrie (Gwendolyn Harris), Jason Flemyng (Jack Napier), Tobias Menzies (Liam Monroe), Christina Chong (Tamsin), James Lance (Connor)

Politics may be a joke to many people, but after a while it stops being funny. Something that comedian Jamie Salter would find out. A previously struggling comedian, Salter voices a cartoon character, Waldo, that specializes in irreverent commentary on social issues and political matters.

Waldo's career begins as the voice of anti-establishment, and anti-status quo. Salter makes a name for the character by trolling politician Liam Monroe, attacking his connections to seedy individuals. He even derails the attempts of Labor MP candidate Gwendolyn Harris in the process. And the people who were fed up with the dysfunction of politics gravitated towards his anti-message. In fact, Waldo became so popular that the team of producers behind him suggested that he run for office as an independent.

Imagine a reality TV star running for public office.

Waldo was a disruptive force in politics and had people enthusiastic about his antics. You might argue too enthusiastic. Exposing his careerist rivals, Waldo became the perfect populist, speaking to the disgust that the everyday person had for the political process. And lost in all the machinations of turning a bit into a brand, Salter winds up a casualty, eventually being replaced and living on the street for speaking up against using Waldo for political manipulation.

"The Waldo Moment" is a Frankenstein story, where the creation gets out of control and becomes something altogether different from what was intended. Here, in Waldo's "don't give a damn" attitude, we can see a similar strain in the candidacy and presidency of Donald Trump. Except this episode predated his campaign by a few years.

Waldo started as a joke, but became a global political brand. Many considered Trump running for President back in 2015 as a joke. And yet look what happened. The shoot from the hip, say whatever you are thinking makes good for entertainment, but not for political office. What started as an absurdity, grew into an eventuality, and many were caught off guard that such an individual could win. And when you embrace the culture of celebrity, hoisting up the wealthy as an example to idolize, then what exactly are you enabling? Modern politics has become just as much of a spectacle as entertainment has, so it was only a matter of time before these two aspects of our society converged.

In that way, "The Waldo Moment" is one of the most predictive episodes in the series, as it foreshadowed the rise of buffoonish politicians like Donald Trump and Boris Johnson. The populism, backed by serious financial interests, was able to use these two as blunt instruments to obstruct any attempts to reform politics. To a great extent, the rise of both politicians were aided by the media, as they built on the willingness to say outrageous things to their audience, and whip up their bases at all cost.

"The Waldo Moment" was meant to be seen as absurd, as something ridiculous that should never happen. The only problem is the joke isn't funny anymore. Because this has become our reality.

Episode 4: White Christmas

Aired: December 16, 2014
Director: Carl Tibbetts
Writer: Charlie Brooker
Cast: John Hamm (as Matthew Trent), Rafe Spall (Joe Potter), Oona Chaplin (Greta), Natalia Tena (Jennifer), Janet Montgomery (Beth), Rasmus Hardiker (Harry)

"My job is to explain to you what is happening as best as I can." –Matthew Trent

Oh wow! A *Black Mirror* Christmas special! We're in for holiday cheer and a light-hearted, feel good story, right? Wrong! "White Christmas" is an interwoven set of three stories, each coming together in the end to culminate into a truly jarring conclusion. By the end, you'll be glad that Christmas only comes once a year.

  The episode begins as Joe Potter wakes up in a strange room. From a frosted window, he appears to be in a remote cabin. There's a picture of a woman next to his room mirror. Walking into the cabin's kitchen, he turns off the radio that had been playing Christmas music. Matthew Trent, supposedly his companion, is already up and working on their Christmas meal.

  Through Matthew, we learn that the two men

have been in the outpost for five years. He tries to make conversation with Joe, but Joe is hesitant to talk. Supposedly, he always had been. Seeing that he was not about to open up, Matthew decides to tell Joe the story about how he wound up in this outpost.

So begins our first of three stories.

Matthew, before his life went downhill, was a dating coach for awkward young men. One of the downsides of technology is that it can, unsurprisingly, hamper one's social skills. And modern problems require modern solutions, right? Capitalizing on this side, Matthew started a side business as a sort of 21st Century Cyrano De Bergerac, using live streaming and an earpiece to directly guide young men on dates. Through a device called the Eye-Link, Matthew helped guys pick clothes, make cold approaches, and coach them into saying the right things at the right times. And it all seemed to be going pretty well.

At least until Harry.

Harry, who Matthew had been helping build up confidence, ends up crashing an office holiday party, where he meets two women, Amy and Jennifer. Using a made up story—one fed to him by Matthew—and a set of photos off of social media, he manages to convince them that he's no stranger and certainly was invited.

If this seems a bit like a jerk move, Matthew says that it's just him watching, but there are in fact eight other men on the line like a Zoom call, co-watching his moves.

Harry starts talking to Amy, but really his goal is Jennifer. Surprisingly it didn't work. Through Matthew's advice, he excuses himself to the restroom to regroup with his guide. When he returns, things go

The Binge Watcher's Guide to Black Mirror

better. He and Jennifer start to talk, and she seems to be on the fence about whether or not to leave her company. Harry talks her into doing it claiming that, essentially, you only live once. Exclaiming that he gets it, she invites him back to her apartment. Score!

Back at her place, Jennifer goes to get two drinks and tells him to head into the bedroom. They each take sips of their drinks, but shortly after Harry starts coughing and asks what was in it. Instead of the sexual encounter that he was expecting, it turns out that Jennifer had been planning to kill herself. She had recently stopped taking her medication, bringing her suicidal thoughts back with their absence.

Meanwhile, Harry is rethinking their entire night. She had said this would be her last Christmas, which he took to mean Christmas party at that particular company. Unfortunately, he found out that she meant last Christmas period. She tells him that she heard him talking to Matthew, and thought that he suffered from the same illness she did—hearing voices and all that. She told him she knew he would understand. But he really didn't.

What was supposed to be a hot date ended up becoming something between a murder and a suicide. Jennifer forces Harry to drink the rest of the deadly concoction and it's over.

Of course, this was all being watched on a live stream by Matthew for eight other guys. And they all just saw a woman murder a love sick young man. In a panic, Matthew tries to wipe all of the evidence—thumb drives, devices, accounts, anything that would lead back to him. But unfortunately, his wife Claire finds out what he was doing, and was not at all happy knowing that he had a role in this. So she ends up blocking him.

Not on social media, but a real life block.

Matthew explains to Joe that—of course due to a set of technological eyes that everyone has—his wife can no longer see or hear him. Try as he might, he cannot interact with her. In addition to that, she leaves him and gets custody of their child. And so Matthew moved to get away from all the reminders of his old life.

Afterwards, Joe becomes a little less tense. He wants to know more. Matthew tells him that the dating service was just a hobby/side gig. His real job was a bit more involved. He begins to tell us our second story about a woman named Greta who had an incredibly complex operation to get herself some additional help.

We see Greta being put under anesthesia and listen as a voice in her head is aware of everything going on. We hear the doctors say "now extracting cookie" and Greta is pulled out, seeing herself lying on the operating table. There is a small extraction wound at the side of her temple, and she appears to be sleeping soundly.

A literal out of body experience, Greta's consciousness has been copied onto a device called a cookie. The cookie—that is a copy of Greta—is then placed by the surgeon into an oval shaped device with a small blue light. Understandably, this is a stressful experience and it's unclear what is occurring.

Matthews job was to do tech support on these "cookies," and to prep them to be useful to the user. At this time, he works for a company called Smartelligence, and he is communicating with Greta's consciousness inside the device. And her first question is one that anyone would ask after something so traumatic. "Am I dead?"

Matthew explains that she is a copy, not the actual Greta. She has no body and is really just code.

The Binge Watcher's Guide to Black Mirror

The real Greta has paid to have her consciousness work as a sort of futuristic virtual assistant. Cookie Greta's role, in this regard, is to do all of the chores for the real Greta's smart home. Matthew then gives her a digital body to help acclimate her to the process.

Directing her attention to a digital control panel, Matthew explains that Cookie Greta has access to the house's temperature, lighting, and is responsible for ordering food. Naturally, expressing human agency, she does not want to do any of this. She screams as she sees her real self taking a nap in the bedroom. So Matthew ends up muting her until she stops.

And this is where it starts to get dark.

After she refuses to do her new job, Matthew does his and sets a timer to make Cookie Greta feel as if three weeks have passed. As nothing more than a program, her perception of time can be manipulated at will. After three weeks of being able to do nothing, not even sleep, Matthew pauses the timer and asks, again, if Cookie Greta is ready to work. She says no, so he sets it to six months. The point is to break the digital version of Greta so she may be useful. Which is exactly what he accomplishes.

By the time the real Greta comes downstairs, her Cookie version is completely broken and ready to run the smart home without any further resistance. We see the Cookie Greta running the automatic toaster and announcing the daily schedule. This is digital slavery and Greta has sold herself into it, in a sense. What else would you call uncompensated and compulsory work? Work that never ends. There are a lot of ethical dilemmas here, which Joe notes as well. He considers it barbaric, and is seen as empathetic by Matthew because of it.

It's then that Joe opens up, telling him about why he was there. He starts off about him and Bethany, an old love interest of his. Things were going okay, but he always knew that her father didn't like him. Further, Joe's drinking habits embarrass Bethany, and visibly so. It was one of those situations that looks good on the surface, but would fracture as their relationship hit bumps in the road.

Joe is cleaning up after a dinner party and finds a positive pregnancy test in the garbage. He asks Beth if it is hers, and she admits it is. Joe is ecstatic, seeing that he's about to be a father. The only problem is that Beth does not want to keep it. They have an argument about it, and Bethany ends up blocking him. The same thing that had happened to Matthew with his wife. He's now nothing but a mute, white outline to her.

The next day, Bethany ends up leaving their apartment while Joe is unable to talk with her in any way because of the block. Wanting to reconcile their relationship, Joe tries waiting outside her job, but never runs into her. Then one day, he sees Bethany's outline, and she's showing. She decided to keep the child. Joe tries to talk to her, but it's on the street and it appears like he is harassing her. This gets him arrested and put under a restraining order. If he violates the order of protection, he goes to prison. Joe spends weeks writing her letters, directed to her father's address, but she never answers.

All he has left are periodic sneak visits to Bethany's father's house, watching from a distance as she and their newborn daughter visit. He can't even see what his daughter looks like, because the block extends to children too. For four years, he visits—

unbeknownst to them— every Christmas Eve. That is, until tragically, Bethany dies in a railroad crash. He finds out watching the news, is able to see her face, because the block comes off when a person dies.

And he realizes he would be able to see his daughter.

Joe takes a trip up to Bethany's father's house and sees his daughter playing with a snowman. But when she turns around, he sees that the child is not his. The father was clearly one of Bethany's co-workers, and Joe is just completely crushed. He goes inside to see Bethany's father, visibly disturbed. He snaps, attacking him with the snow globe he had bought as a gift for his daughter. And in that spur of anguish, kills him.

A few days later, Bethany's daughter tries to go get help, but doesn't make it far in the deep snow. And so the little girl ends up freezing to death just a few yards away from her granddad's house.

Joe is responsible for the deaths of two people, and Matthew—who turns out to not be a co-worker—was really there to get him to confess. After he gets what he needs, he says out loud that, "I'm coming out now." The whole time, they had been inside of a simulation. Further, it's revealed that Joe is actually a cookie that was extracted and placed in this digital cabin. The time adjustment machine made it feel like five years for Joe, but Matthew was only working on his case for a little over an hour! Meanwhile, the real Joe was in a prison cell and is informed that his cookie has confessed to the murders.

And Matthew had extracted his confession in exchange for his own freedom for the events of the first story. However, since he is considered a sex offender, the police tell him that he is blocked by everyone. Doomed to being a practical ghost for the rest of his life. Matthew steps outside, and all he sees are white outlines all around him. This was the true meaning of "White Christmas." His outline appears red to everyone else, denoting his status as a peeper. It's like a digital scarlet letter for the world to see.

As for Joe's cookie, he was still stranded in that simulation. The police set his time rate to 1000 years per minute, and leave him on for the duration of Christmas. We see the Cookie Joe stuck in the same cabin he killed Bethany's father in, repeatedly slamming a radio on the ground. And each time he did, the same radio would appear, playing the same song even louder. He has to listen to Christmas music for what seems like an eternity. A super cruel ending. *Black Mirror* tends to have a lot of those.

Naturally, there are a number of ethical concerns here. The big question is whether or not cookies count as sentient forms of life. Also, is it right to cause harm to a copy of a person? Is it ethical to inflict suffering for the purpose of justice? Is this yet another example of cruel and unusual punishment, from a technological standpoint? The ethical dimensions here are wide.

Whether we like to admit it or not, our society's concept of punishment emerges from the religious concept of eternal damnation. Further, the police extract false confessions from people more often than we would like to admit. The idea of law enforcement being able to extract a confession from an abused digital version, and have it stick to the real living person is outright terrifying. Who is to say that this won't be abused in the future?

Season 3

Episode 1: Nosedive

Aired: October 21, 2016
Director: Joe Wright
Writer: Charlie Brooker
Cast: Bryce Dallas Howard (as Lacie Pound), Alice Eve (Naomie Blestow), Cherry Jones (Susan), James Norton (Bryan Pound), Michaela Coel (Airport Stewardess), Kadiff Kirwan (Chester)

"I didn't even do anything!" – Lacie Pound

It's so easy to fall out of favor, something social climber and people-pleaser Lacie Pound finds out the hard way in "Nosedive." Lacie wants to improve her life, and the only way to do so is to boost her social score. Picture a society where every interaction you have with someone is rated, and based on that rating, your life can be easier or harder. For example, Lacie is after a nicer apartment, but can only get one by having her score go up.

In our opening scene, we see Lacie go for a jog in her suburban neighborhood, an earpiece and phone in her hand. Now, this is not out of the ordinary even today, but we might notice something a bit different as she passes a group of runners. Rather than just waving, she points her phone at a guy who says hello to her, and there's this little notification sound. In that quick moment, their interaction has been rated. And of course he quickly rates her as well.

She stops for a brief moment, just long enough to take a picture of herself, post workout. While scrolling through an app on her phone that shows a timeline of her friends, we see that there is also a way to rate photos with stars. The max is five.

As someone who is fully immersed in this new world, Lacie is a play-by-the-rules kind of person. Which at times can mean playing along, even when you don't necessarily feel like it. We watch as she practices her laugh in the bathroom mirror, trying to get it to be acceptable and "right" for any occasion. A cornea implant lights up, and her social rating appear in the mirror—a 4.2. A good score, but not quite enough to get where she wants to go.

This rating system is everywhere—compulsory and inescapable. While waiting in line for tea and a cookie, Lacie is scrolling her timeline and rating every picture with the goal of getting rated back positively. She rates the man who serves her, and he responds in kind. It's like Yelp, but for people.

Later, in the elevator with a co-worker, we see Lacie use her phone to pull up information via her eye implant to make small talk. Beth is higher rated than her and is starting a new job. A job that is on one of the top floors in the same building. It's not stated directly, but it's implied that a better social score means more opportunities to move up and move on.

Lacie is still at her current job, but says that it's fine for now. While she's at work we see her constantly scrolling and liking pictures on her timeline. The app looks like some rough combination of Facebook and Instagram, complete with video features. Lacie focuses in on the timeline of one of her oldest friends, Naomi. Naomi is rated as a 4.8. She looks at a doll that is on her desk, but is interrupted by one of her co-workers, Chester.

This is where it gets interesting. Chester, who is visibly nervous, offers Lacie a green smoothie. He bought one for her, and everybody else at the job. Chester is a 3.1 and obviously doing all he can to stay in everyone's good graces. Lacie up-rates Chester—to his relief—but her co-workers all look at her sideways for doing so. See, when Chester broke up with another co-worker everyone sided with Gordon.

Here we find out the dark side of this social rating system. If you fall out of favor, your score can come down real quick. Lacie even learns that if Chester falls below a 2.5, he can lose his job. What's being likable have to do with being good at your job? After explaining to Lacie what happens, one of her co-workers pulls out his phone and down rates Chester.

The social rating system can be weaponized to put people on the outs, and fast. And Lacie would find that out as she was given three anonymous down votes after the interaction. This was her punishment for violating the workplace clique arrayed against Chester. This is technologically enabled pettiness, and these dings she receives are a portion of what is to come.

Still apartment hunting, Lacie visits a nearby building with vacancies. The broker shows her a nice, luxury apartment, pre-loaded with exercise equipment and well out of her price range. The broker tells her about the Prime Influencers Program, and how it can save her on the cost, but she needs to be at least a 4.5. Taken aback by this, she decides to meet with an agent.

The company is called Reputelligent and it does social credit counseling for your profile. The agent explains that Lacie needs scores from higher rated people in order to climb any further than she has. On her way to work the next morning, she encounters Chester who has apparently fallen below 2.5. The door won't even open for him, and security is standing by looking irate. He asks Lacie to up-rate him, but she refuses and brushes by as if she doesn't know him. He is ostracized, and to help him would mean harming her reputation in the process.

Determined to find a way to boost her score, she focuses on her highly rated friend Naomi. The doll that she has on her desk at work, Mr. Rags, was something the two of them had shared as little girls. She takes a picture of the doll and uploads it to her account, to which Naomi sees almost immediately and rates it 4.8 stars.

Afterwards, Naomi gives her a video call, and talks about how much that share of Mr. Rags meant to her. They have known each other since they were five years old, but it's hard to keep in touch as you get older. She invites Lacie to be at her wedding as the maid of honor. Naomi is going to get married at a private island, and wants Lacie to be there. What better way to boost your social score than attending a wedding of all highly ranked people? Lacie of course accepts immediately and begins to plan.

Her brother Ryan—the voice of reason—reminds Lacie that Naomi was always mean to her, and even slept with a guy she was interested in back in their day. As a brother, he is trying to warn her about losing

The Binge Watcher's Guide to Black Mirror

herself in this chase for bigger and better things, but Lacie doesn't want to hear it. In spite of the questionable things that her "friend" has done, Lacie intends to go to the wedding, give her speech, and get the boost that she needs. This is a transaction and she's fully aware of that reality.

Now, instead of seeing Lacie make it to the wedding without incident, and getting everything she wants, in typical *Black Mirror* fashion everything goes south pretty quickly. Firstly, after an argument with her brother, Lacie misses her cab to the airport. The driver down rates Lacie for the snub, and she has to call for another. Next, she bumps into a woman and makes her spill the coffee she was holding. She quickly down-rates Lacie, and it appears that down rates from people with higher scores hit harder. To make it worse, the guy driving the cab—who was visibly annoyed with Naomi and Lacie's phone call in the cab—one stars her. Ouch.

When Lacie gets to the airport, we see the social consequences of this rating system. Her previous flight was canceled, and the only seat on a flight leaving that evening is available to 4.2s and better. Because of the earlier incidents down-rating her, Lacie is now only a mere 4.1. Understandably upset, she gets into a disagreement with the customer service rep. Brilliantly played by Michaela Cole, the check-in representative was having none of Lacie's verbal abuse. Calling airport security, Lacie's score falls even further. And with a smile on his face, airport security down-rates her a whole point, putting her at a 3.1

And to make matters worse, any additional negative feedback for the remainder of the night will result in her losing double the points she would normally lose. While it's only temporary, it is extremely punitive and means that she can't catch the flight at all. She is told to vacate the premises.

Lacie now has to rent an electric car and drive to Naomi's wedding. But of course, when she gets to the rental place, all that is available to her is an older model that she is surprised is even still in production. It wasn't even fully charged when the place let her rent it. Now she has to pull into a station and charge her car, but it's an old model. The charging station doesn't even take the charger and Lacie needs a converter.

Desperate to make it to her friend's wedding—and repair her score—she starts walking down the highway trying to hitchhike. At this point, her score is so low that people drive by not wanting to help. They think she must have done something, and thus want nothing to do with her. One of the motorists even anonymously down-rates her, to which Lacie exclaims, "I didn't even do anything!" Eventually, a truck driver named Susan pulls up to help. She's a 1.4.

During the ride, she tells Lacie how she became a 1.4. Apparently, she used to be a 4.6, but lost her husband to cancer. The issue was that, the hospital gave the one open bed to a 4.4 and Susan's husband was a 4.3. After he died, she just lost it and dropped the façade. Susan started saying whatever she wanted, when she wanted, regardless of how people would feel about it. She talks about how liberating it was to do that, and how people really aren't here for total honesty. Susan recommends that Lacie do the same, but she has no such intention.

This conversation here is really telling. When

Susan asks Lacie exactly what it is she's after playing this social game, she can't really explain it very well. It's just a social expectation. It's indicative of the rat race that many of us are in, that no one asked to be a part of and no one knows how to stop participating.

The next morning, as they get close to her destination, Susan leaves her a red thermos filled with whiskey. Juxtaposed with an earlier offer of a blue thermos of coffee, it's a low key reference to The Matrix, with Susan offering Lacie an escape from this merry go round of social score clout chasing.

While practicing her speech in a rest-stop bathroom, Lacie overhears two fans of a fictional science fiction show, "Seas of Tranquility", headed to Port Mary. She quickly searches up the show on her phone and tells them that her friend has her costume, and she was on her way to the same convention, but her car broke down. Happy to help a fellow fan, they agree to let her catch a ride with them. Everyone there is dressed up like a character from the show, and Lacie is looking suspect. When one of them asks who her favorite character is, she gets the question wrong. They let her slide, at least until she takes a phone call. It's from Naomi.

Her score has fallen so low at this point that Naomi has decided to uninvite her. She has a reputation and a score of her own to protect after all. Just an hour away from the wedding, Lacie is now a 2.6 and her presence there would be bad for Naomi. No surprise, it was a numbers game for them both. The downside of transactional friendships are really brought out here. They argue, and she calls Lacie out for pretending that it was not about boosting her score up as well. Both were using each other, and never really friends.

However, Lacie is still planning to give her speech, and decides to crash Naomi's wedding. After getting hung up on, Lacie just outright admits that she's never watched the show and even insults it. Which of course gets her unceremoniously kicked off the RV, and down-rated. Why she didn't just play along for the next hour or so until they got there, I don't get. But okay. She's on that Susan route now.

Lacie pops open that red thermos and guzzles down the whiskey on the side of the road. She's not about to turn back now. She manages to borrow a guy's motorbike and rides the rest of the way there. Then, while looking for an alternative entrance, falls off the bike and splashes into the mud. The phrase "my name is mud" comes to mind.

Lacie crashes the wedding, and somehow manages to give her speech. Except it's less a speech, and more a nervous breakdown in front of all of Naomi's new friends. Reminiscing, and lamenting their friendship, she points out all of the things that her brother Ryan had said about Naomi. She has a full-scale meltdown at this point, is thrown out by security, and arrested.

At the police station, the cornea implants are removed and she is placed in a cell. Lacie has lost everything that mattered to her in the matter of hours. This includes her job, her best friend, and her shot at living in a luxury apartment. It's questionable as to whether or not she has lost her mind as well. Interestingly enough, when Lacie looks around her cell, she looks as if she is seeing things as they are for the first time.

While in her cell, Lacie sees another man across from her, staring. Obviously, the guy has had the same thing happen to him. Lacie tells the guy to stop looking at her, but he does not. Instead, they start clowning each other about what they have on. They go back and forth, roasting each other with mean spirited jokes. Except they're smiling the entire time, finally free to just say whatever is on their mind without consequence.

This episode really captures how social media can feed into being self-absorbed and myopic. When only your immediate concerns matter, its encapsulated in what is referred to now as main character syndrome. Lacie wound up worse off than some of the people she refused to help. There are lessons here about the tyranny of the majority, social conformity, and even cancel culture. It appears that though we are connected, technology has given us new ways to fall out.

In what is, admittedly one of my favorite episodes, we see Lacie attempt to play the game, only to end up with the game playing her. It goes to show that a whole lot of social niceties are not genuine, and that friendship is such a flimsy thing nowadays. Naomi went all Mean Girls on Lacie at the mere thought of her score dropping. In this world of digitally refined classism, "Nosedive" shows what society could become. China is already working on a social credit system, which tracks reputation and can include personal behaviors like jaywalking.

The colorful and inviting world depicted in this *Black Mirror* episode is, in actuality, a prison of other people's opinions. People generally want to be seen doing the right thing, even if it is not who they really are. This episode made a big impact and is still a doozy to re-watch. It generalized how people with bad credit are treated, and broadened it to social media.

Could you imagine what your score would be if you said something positive about a widely hated person? Or, imagine getting down-rated just because someone doesn't like your face.

The way a bad Yelp review could financially hurt a business, this in the same way dings on a future social credit system that could ruin people's lives. Not a very nice thought, is it? If this nightmare of a rating system ever comes to pass here, it would be the end of so many people. I would just start posting only photos of kittens, roses, and good morning messages. Anything else would be far too risky. Be careful with your opinions—others might not like them and digitally punish you for it. Have a nice day!

Episode 2: Playtest

Aired: October 21, 2016
Director: Dan Trachtenburg
Writer: Charlie Brooker
Cast: Wyatt Russell (As Cooper Redfield), Hannah **John**-Kamen (Sonja), Wunmi Mosaku (Katie), Ken Yamamura (Shou Saito), Elizabeth Moynihan (Cooper's Mom)

"Get out of my head!" – Cooper Redfield

So, you like video games, do you? So you'd like to test them out, for free, wouldn't you? Cooper Redfield gets his chance in "Playtest." Cooper, a well-traveled young man happens upon an opportunity to test out a new game. At first it seems like it's not a big deal, except that there is no console, nor controller. And this is *Black Mirror*.

A year before we meet him, Cooper's father passes away and he is doing his best to live an adventurous life while he can. Even if that means being away from home, and his still grieving mother. In the wee hours of the morning, he sneaks out to go jet setting around the world. In the cab, he gets a call from his mom, but doesn't pick up.

Cooper is a traveling man, bouncing from country to country to see as much of the world as he can. He's visited Australia, Thailand, India, Italy, Spain, and finally Britain. There, he meets up with his friend Sonja at a bar and tells her of his travels. This was supposed to be the last part of his trip before he headed home, and he wanted some suggestions about fun things to do. He got it. After learning he was going home next week, Sonja and Cooper hook up.

Cooper wakes up at Sonja's place and he avoids two additional calls from his mom. He admits that he's avoiding her calls, explaining that he doesn't want to open a can of worms. Opening up to Sonja, he tells her about his father who passed away of Alzheimer's Disease, and that he had been taking care of him up until that point. Alzheimer's is a neurodegenerative disease that gradually destroys the sufferer's memory, motor functions, and there is no cure.

He mentions to Sonja that there were times that his father would look at him and not know who he was. And unfortunately, Alzheimer's is also hereditary. Which is why Cooper wants to have as many experiences as he can, while he can. As for his mother, he knows that he needs to address it, but would rather do it when he gets back to the United States. Sonja lends a sympathetic ear to Cooper, and encourages him to call his mom. We see him try, but his anxiety gets the best of him and he just couldn't bring himself to do it.

In the next scene, Cooper tries to withdraw money for a ticket back home, but has insufficient funds. He calls the bank to find that someone used his account to make a purchase in another country. One that drained what little money he had.

The Binge Watcher's Guide to Black Mirror

Momentarily stuck in Britain—and strapped for cash—Cooper decides to pick up an odd job to help pay for his plane ticket. Sonja points out a paying opportunity for a game tester from Saito Gaming, who is testing a new survival horror game. She shows him a magazine with the founder of Saito on the cover which notably features a lead story about TCKR—another mention that will be important in future episodes. Cooper decides to follow through, both for the easy cash, and to help Sonja who is a tech journalist. She asks him to take a picture of the tech they use, which he agrees in exchange for her help.

Cooper ventures off to Saito Gaming's headquarters, located in a very remote part of the country. He meets Katie, who is there to walk him through the process. There are posters for games like Skinned Alive and Harlech Shadows, the survival horror game that Sonja mentioned to him. Escorted to an empty white room, he is asked to relinquish his phone. Also, he has to sign a non-disclosure agreement. Cooper jokes about having his kidneys harvested, but he doesn't have any idea what he is in for.

The twist is that this game is based on your memories. What he thought would be a normal game test, Cooper hesitates when he is told that it will involve a small medical procedure. It's explained to him that the procedure is no more invasive then having his ears pierced, and he decides to do it. Katie forgets the signature page, and the moment she leaves the room, Cooper turns his phone on to take a picture of the set up. He sends it via text to Sonja.

If you look closely at the gaming set up in the briefcase that Cooper opens, you can see the White

Bear symbol. While the episodes aren't connected, *Black Mirror* likes to drop interconnected references here and there. Katie comes back with the signature page sooner than Cooper was prepared for, and he forgets to turn his phone off. Once he signs, they proceed to set up the test.

Cooper is told that it is an augmented reality game, layered over our physical reality. Seated in his chair, he's connected to a headset across his temple. Katie then pulls out a device called a "mushroom" that plugs into the back of his neck. It's not permanent, only there to connect him to the augmented reality. Katie lays out five circular pads in front of Cooper, and then begins initializing the program. While that is happening, his phone rings, and once again it's his mom. Katie sees this and turns it off.

They begin the first version of the trial, where the pads turn into holes with a little digital mole that only Cooper can see. The mole is a projection coming from his implant, and as he proceeds to play digital whack a mole, he's thrilled. But that was just a demo. Katie tells him about the possibility of testing the full experience, which having got a little taste, he is up for. And of course, there is more money on the line.

In the next scene, Katie introduces Cooper to Shou Saito, the head of the company. Shou wanes philosophical about how gaming can be good for you, and how it gives everyone different experiences. He asks why scaring people has such an impact, and Cooper answers the adrenaline rush that comes after it. Shou talks about the benefits of facing your greatest fears in a safe environment and explains that they are working on a personal survival horror game—one that uses your own memories to try and scare you. Katie connects an additional piece to Cooper's mushroom called a neural net package—an AI system that monitors your brain activity to adjust to what gets a scare out of you. They upload the software, and Cooper stands up, seemingly normal. Katie and Shou have done this before, and look at him somewhat nervously before he says he's fine and ready to play.

Cooper is escorted via car to an old, 19th Century style house. He recognizes it as the Harlech Shadow house. The goal of the game is for him to spend as long as he can there, despite surviving the horrors that the AI would pull from his mind. Seems simple enough, right? They give him an earpiece to contact Katie in case he needs to, but he is told that nothing there can physically harm him, and that he can be pulled out whenever he wants. It's like having a safe word, but for a video game. Cooper agrees, and is left alone in the house.

With his phone back at Saito Gaming, and the house having no internet, Cooper picks up a book, and starts reading. It's *The Raven* by Edgar Allen Poe. It's not long until he sees a spider crawling around the carpet. He winces a little bit, losing sight of it before it appears on the arm of the chair he's sitting on. Spooked, he jumps up and looks around for it. Cooper is scared of spiders, and the AI program pulled that from his mind. Katie, who is monitoring him, laughs at his fear of spiders. Cooper downplays it by saying that he is not fond of them, that's all.

Soon after, Cooper spots a difference in the portrait of the house. He notices now that there is a light on, and a guy standing in the window. Looking away for a moment, it disappears. Nervous laughter on his part ensues, soon followed by footsteps upstairs. He downplays it, sure that it's just leaky pipes. He turns around only to face a man dressed in 19th Century clothing. But Cooper recognizes him immediately as Josh Peters, the guy who bullied him in high school. He admits that this one got him going. Knowing that it's just a hologram, Cooper jokes about if he knew Krav Maga, he would have been able to defend himself as a kid. Every bullied kid has been there, replaying what they could have done differently in the past.

Still communicating with Katie, he goes for ginger snaps in the cupboards. He expects Josh Peters to be right behind the cupboard when he closes the door, but gets something worse. He sees a shadow of Peters that disappears, only to be replaced by a giant spider crawling towards him. The freaky bit is that the spider has Josh Peters' face. He describes what he sees to Katie over the earpiece, but communication has been lost.

There's a loud knock at the door, and he assumes its Katie and tech support coming to fix the earpiece. But when he opens the door, it's Sonja. She tells him that he is in danger. He reaches out to touch Sonja, and sees that she is actually there, and she explains that tourists have been disappearing because of this game company. But Cooper doesn't buy it.

He asks Sonja how she found out where he was, to which she says that she tracked his phone. However, his phone is back at Saito Gaming, and Sonja is busted. Brushing past him, she goes to the kitchen drawer and tells him that she hacked his bank account, cloning his card while he was asleep. Sonja turns around, with a big butcher knife in her hand and admits that she lead him to this place, and that he should have called his mom. Cooper backs away, pleading with her to put the knife down. He turns to run, but the Peters spider appears in front of him, while Sonja stabs him in the back. Cooper feels actual pain, despite being told nothing could harm him.

They struggle for a while and he throws her into the cabinet. Sonja gets back up, and attacks again. Wrestling him to the floor, she forces the knife to go through the front of his shoulder. Cooper pulls at her face to find a red skeleton underneath. Not knowing what the hell is going on, he grabs Sonja by the head, and plunges it into the knife protruding from his shoulder. He's on the floor, screaming in pain and at this point scared out of his mind. Or, more precisely, scared because of his mind. He then sees that everything has vanished—Sonja, the butcher knife, everything, and his earpiece is now working.

Katie tells him that physical sensations should not be possible. Maybe this was something they discovered by accident. After all, some of the biggest scientific studies and technological breakthroughs often happen by accident. Unfortunately, Cooper was the test subject and he wants to exit the game. He is so freaked out that he threatens to pull the mushroom out of the back of his head. Katie warns him that it could kill him and talks him down from doing that, explaining that he has to get to the access point to leave. All he has to do is go upstairs and open a door, but he is afraid that the AI will present him with a scenario where he comes into the room and see his mom dead. But it's the only way.

Once he opens the door, Katie tells him there was no access point at all. He turns back around to see that the door is gone. No way back now. It's here where Katie starts bombarding him with questions that he can't answer. This program was taking his memories, much like his late Alzheimer's stricken father. It tapped into his worse fear, and used it against him.

Cooper breaks the mirror that he is looking at, angry that he's not able to recognize himself. And just as he takes one of the shards of glass—with the intention of cutting the mushroom out of the back of his neck—security guards rush in to see that he doesn't, along with Katie and Shou. Katie is carrying the laptop with the initiating sequence, but is apparently unable to stop it. Cooper looks at both of them, unsure of who they are.

And Shou says "put him with the others."

Cooper yells "stop" several times and is awakened by Katie pulling the mushroom out of the back of his neck. He's still sitting in the chair at Saito Gaming and was told he was only in the game for one second.

Shaken, Cooper heads back home. On the flight back, everything seems normal, but back home, when he goes upstairs to his mom's room, she is there and doesn't recognize him. She says to him "I have to call him" not realizing that her son is right there in front of her. Cooper is witnessing the same thing happen to his mother that happened to his father. And we see him calling to his mother over and over again in anguish.

The scene cuts back to Cooper, still in the chair at Saito, and something has gone horribly wrong. The phone he wasn't supposed to have rings, interfering with the upload signal. Ultimately, it lit up all of his synapses and killed him. And the last thing he yelled was "Mom."

Men often call for their mothers when they are on the verge of dying. It happens in wars, on battlefields, and we revert to children and call on the one who brought us into this world. The test only lasted for a few seconds, but all of this occurred in Cooper's mind. A poor fellow with unresolved trauma who did not have the chance to make amends with his mom. He was pretty much a guinea pig.

There is a real game called S*ilent Hill: Shattered Memories* that psychologically profiles you to learn your behaviors. The game at the time even came with a psychology warning. It warned that: "This video game psychologically profiles you as you play. It gets to know who you really are then uses that information to change itself. It uses its knowledge against you, creating your own personal nightmare. This game plays you as much as you play it."

Playtest is pretty much this concept expounded upon into an entire episode. It has a lot of eerie feelings to it, and holds up really well even with multiple viewings. There are a lot of themes here about unresolved issues and unconscious fears. Overall, this episode is a total mind fuck. Once games stop having controllers and consoles, I might have to be done with gaming. There is escapism, but this is not it. This would not be the last episode that will show an augmented reality game, and it lays the foundation for the future gaming related episodes.

It's just too bad for Cooper that he never had a chance to re-spawn. Game over.

Episode 3: Shut Up And Dance"

Aired: October 21, 2016
Director: James Watkins
Writer: Charlie Brooker and William Bridges
Cast: Alex Lawther (Kenny), Jerome Flynn (Hector), Susannah Doyle (Blackmailed Woman), Frankie Wilson (Tom), Jimmy Roye-Dunne (Red), Hannah Steele (Melissa)

"There's no cure for the internet."- Hector

There truly is a dark side to the internet. We live in a time where pretty much anyone can be the blackmailed—a harsh reality that Kenny and others would find out in "Shut Up And Dance."

Kenny is your typical teenager with a menial job and not a lot of friends. He's the butt of jokes at work and he just has to suck it up. At home, he retreats into his laptop to listen to music and just diddle around the web. Bored, alone, and with no prospects for a girlfriend, Kenny finds a pornographic video and beats off.

A few moments later however, Kenny receives an anonymous email in all caps: "WE SAW WHAT YOU DID." His laptop camera was off, but as many people know, it can still be remotely activated. Terrified, he asks who they are, but they instead demand he send his cell phone number, or else they will leak the video of him masturbating to all of his email contacts. Understandably shaken, Kenny complies.

Afterwards, he receives a text saying that soon he will be activated, and that he has to remain on standby. Kenny has just found himself entrapped by a hacker, and is on the hook for the remainder of the episode. But that's not all. There's more. There are other people who have been similarly ensnared.

Kenny is ordered to deliver a cake to a random man in a hotel room. Hector—the man in question—is looped in by the hackers to accept the cake, and drive with Kenny to a bank. Hector is being blackmailed, because he was supposed to meet a prostitute at the hotel. They are told to dig inside the cake where they find a gun, a baseball cap, and a pair of shades. There are further instructions to rob the bank, and decide who will be the robber and who the getaway driver. Kenny is hesitant, but Hector asserts that he has to do this or he'll lose everything and pressures him to do the job. They rob the bank and take the money to a public place for drop off.

This episode ends in a really nihilistic fashion. Instead of everyone getting what they want and being left alone to live their lives, the network of hackers ends up releasing their information anyway. They did all of it, just because they could. Everyone's life is blown up, and they all are confronted with the consequences. There is a dark, humorous undertone to all of this, because we're watching it happen to someone else. But would we feel the same sense of justice if it happened to us? We also find out that poor innocent Kenny, who we were rooting for to get off the hook because all he did was jerk off, had actually been looking at underage girls. *Black Mirror* is good for throwing you a loop with their main characters.

Every one of the victims were looped into this for something they have done online, most of which would rarely ever come to light. Imagine having to explain your most strange web searches, or what you said about someone else online. "Shut Up and Dance" shows that, like it or not, no one's hands are clean. In fact, many normal looking people might have very dark secrets.

This ending never sat well with me, and I realize that it's not meant to sit well with anyone. That's kind of the point. In real life, even online interactions can have real world consequences. Could you imagine if we had to answer for every single thing we did online?

I believe that is the message here. If your behavior offline and online don't align, then change for the better. Or else some hacker collective is going to scoop your personal details and ruin your life. What a comforting thought, huh?

Episode 4: San Junipero

Aired: October 21, 2016
Director: Owen Harris
Writer: Charlie Brooker
Cast: Gugu Mbatha-Raw (As Kelly Booth), Mackenzie Davis (Yorkie), Denise Burse (Elder Kelly), Annabel Davis (Elder Yorkie), Raymond McAnally (Greg), Gavin Stenhouse (Wes)

"You want to spend forever somewhere nothing matters?" -Kelly

The idea of eternal love is strong in the human imagination. But in the future, with technological assistance, love can last forever. Set in 1987, "San Junipero" at its heart is a love story between two women, and what happens after we pass on. Of course, this is *Black Mirror*, so things aren't quite so straight forward.

A very reserved Yorkie meets Kelly for the first time at a club called Tuckers. She initially shows no interest in any of the guests, walking through the crowd to visit the arcade portion. While she's playing, a man tries repeatedly to strike up conversation with her. He goes on about how the game she's playing has different endings, and it breaks her concentration, resulting in a loss. He asks her if she wants to play with him, but she's not interested at all.

Yorkie excuses herself, choosing to sit alone on a sofa and enjoy her drink. At the same time, Kelly is trying to ditch her own admirer and decides the best way to it is to act like she is catching up with an old friend. Asking Yorkie to go along with whatever she says, she makes up a story about how her friend only has six months to live.

After both men disappear, Kelly introduces herself and invites Yorkie to have a drink at the bar. They talk for a bit and Yorkie mentions that she's not from San Junipero. Their chat is punctuated by "Fake," a song by Alexander O'Neal, and Kelly wants to hit the dance floor. That was a serious jam. Visibly uncomfortable, Yorkie tags along.

While Kelly is carefree and outgoing—and extra showy on the dance floor—Yorkie on the other hand is self-conscious, and just kind of there. She's not accustomed to having a whole bunch of eyes on her. Her social anxiety is so intense at that point she decides to leave the dance floor to go sit down outside. Kelly follows her and invites Yorkie to sleep with her. While tempted, Yorkie has a fiancée—Greg—and declines. Noting that it's getting late, Yorkie says she should get going and walks off in the rain. She was just not ready for Kelly.

A week later, Yorkie returns to Tuckers where Wes is still borderline harassing Kelly for another date. She explains that she doesn't want anything serious or long term, and that their encounter two weeks ago may have been a connection to him, but just sex to her. She encourages him to go find another girl in San Junipero, and bids him farewell.

Yorkie shows up a few moments after, but Kelly is already with some other guy. She's listening to him drone on about his old wounds as a surfer dude, but she's looking at Yorkie from across the room. Excusing herself to go to the bathroom, she meets Yorkie in the bathroom. Yorkie is with it this week. They end up leaving the club together and head back to Kelly's. They sleep with one another.

In the afterglow, they talk about their past experiences. Yorkie reveals that she has never been with anyone before, and Kelly reveals that she used to be married to a guy, but never acted on any of her inward feelings towards women. She says he chose not to stick around, and now Kelly is all about having a good time. A tear falls from her eyes when she talks about it, and Yorkie wipes it away.

Next week, Yorkie shows up at Tuckers, but does not see Kelly at all. After speaking with the bartender, she heads to another club—The Quagmire—in hopes of seeing her. The Quagmire is one of those anything goes type of places, and Yorkie has to wade through a crowd of goths, a dominatrix, and some caged Fight Club type situation. She's completely out of her element. While there, she bumps into Wes, who recognizes her from Tuckers. Yorkie asks him if Kelly had been here, but he says she hasn't. He figures out that Kelly had her way with Yorkie, and says "You too, huh?" Before Yorkie walks off, Wes tells her to try a different time. It's here, that we start to see one twist.

This episode, strangely enough, jumps across different decades, with Yorkie looking to reconnect with Kelly over the 80's, 90's and 2000's. Eventually she realizes that she's been ghosted. The next week, Yorkie emerges in 1980 with no sight of Kelly. The week after that, it's 1996. Same club, different decade. Except, instead of Pac-Man, someone is playing Time Crisis. Next week, it's Tuckers in 2002 where, finally, Yorkie sees Kelly. She's in the arcade playing Dance Dance Revolution, in high heels. That's impressing to witness. And Kelly is not thrilled to see her. She walks off to take a bathroom break, but Yorkie follows, asking why she just disappeared on her like that.

Kelly doesn't even feel bad about ghosting Yorkie, since she's just about having fun, and reiterates that fact. Yorkie berates her and walks off, leaving a frustrated Kelly who shatters the bathroom mirror. She looks down at her hand to see that it's not wounded, and looks back up at the mirror to see that it is no longer broken. Now we know for sure that this is not real life. The reason they can jump from decade to decade each week, is because it is a simulation. Participants are able to immerse themselves in a world where it was a part of their lifetime.

When Kelly goes to talk to Yorkie on the rooftop, she mentions something about pain-sliders. Kelly is about to apologize, but Yorkie interrupts her and asks the pivotal question. She asks how many of the residents of San Junipero are dead. Kelly says 80 to 85 percent.

Behind all of the evasion, and the non-committal attitude, we find out the truth of what San Junipero is. San Junipero is a life simulation program for aging people. Kelly and Yorkie are both participants in this immersive world, but constrained to five hours a week, on Saturday nights. Kelly has taken the trial run, but doesn't plan on sticking around. The full timers that she refers to are the people who have decided to have their digital consciousness preserved after they die. They live forever in this computer simulation and make up the majority of its population.

While Kelly is enjoying it, she doesn't want to stay. Even with three months to live, San Junipero is not the place for her. She is thinking of her late husband Richard, who had the chance to take it, but decided not to. So that's what she meant by he didn't want to stick around. Here, we have the concept of a digital afterlife. This revelation in itself is a trip enough as it is.

What's more, is that both Kelly and Yorkie are using avatars. When they decide to meet up in real life, Kelly is in her early 70's and resides in an assisted living facility. Yorkie on the other hand, is a bed-ridden quadriplegic with a tracheostomy tube. While she can hear Kelly, she can't respond. On her visit, Kelly runs into the real life Greg, who is one of the nurses at the facility where Yorkie resides. He tells her how it happened.

Yorkie came out to her parents when she was 21, causing a fight. Upset, Yorkie gets in her car and drives off, but gets into an accident that put her in the condition she is in. And that was 40 years ago. This system was a second chance for her, and is why it was so important.

Greg can communicate with her via the comm box, and is marrying Yorkie so that she can pass over, as she is not legally allowed to make those decisions for herself. Kelly, in turn, pleads with Greg to connect her to San

Junipero, which he agrees to, but only for five minutes. Kelly logs on, and meets Yorkie. Understanding the full weight of the situation, Kelly asks Yorkie to marry her instead, and she accepts. After spending some time together, Kelly digitally signs the agreement to allow Yorkie to pass over, and her life support systems are suspended. She is gone in the flesh, but now living in the cloud.

We next see Yorkie on the beach in San Junipero, letting the waves wash over her. She is thrilled that she truly lives there now, experiencing everything that she had missed out on for the past 40 years. The feeling of sand in her toes, looking at the sunset, going for a joy ride in a jeep—things we take for granted. She asks Kelly to join her, meaning upload herself to the cloud as well. Except Kelly still doesn't want to. Yorkie brings up Kelly's late husband Richard, and that's when she goes off.

Kelly mentions their life together, and that they were together for 49 years. They had a daughter who passed away at only 39. Richard didn't want to stay, because the technology didn't exist for his daughter to do the same. His religious beliefs about the afterlife didn't help either. Because of this, Kelly is adamant about not sticking around. To stay, while her husband and daughter did not, rubs her the wrong way. The clock strikes 12, and their time ends. Kelly is booted from San Junipero, leaving Yorkie there by herself.

In the real world, Kelly gets sicker as time goes on. Her cancer is spreading, and she is down to a few weeks left at best. And right at the end of it all, she actually changes her mind, deciding to stay in San Junipero. In real life, she's euthanized and buried in a plot with her husband and daughter. In the program, Kelly surprises Yorkie, and they are reunited, their digital consciousnesses together forever, in the cloud. And the same song that started the episode, ends it—"Heaven is a Place on Earth" by Belinda Carlisle. So appropriate. While this episode can be very emotional to watch at the end, it is one of the very few stories in this anthology that have an actual happy ending.

There is so much to observe about this episode. For those who believe in a person having a soul, is it wrong to upload your consciousness into virtual reality to cheat death? Is a replica of your consciousness, and all of your memories, equivalent to being a fully-fledged human being?

But that's not what it's really about.

San Junipero is a love story about second chances. Yorkie, who became quadriplegic 40 years ago, was given a chance to live, albeit digitally. Themes about freedom to be who you are, and love who you want are strong here. There is also a lot to be said about the way that ageism and appearance based discrimination put severe limitations on the lives of many. This inspiring episode is showing the possibility of being free of all of that.

The musical selections in this episode are just everything. They were so deep, that when the episode came out, there was actually a San Junipero soundtrack released. It's still up on Spotify, if you want to check it out. And why not? Get some of that old school music in your ears. Okay, I'm geeking out here. My bad!

This episode will cause a whole lot of nostalgia for those who remember songs from this era. Both people who grew up in the 80's, and people who still value the musicians of that time. The songs from Alexander O'Neal, Belinda Carlisle, among others are just so great to hear, and re-introduce them to a younger audience. I found myself searching up all of the songs that played during this episode, going down memory lane. Even the games, whether it's Bubble Bobble or Pac-Man, make me nostalgic for that time of the world.

It's like someone decided to take the computer game Second Life, and make it into a fully immersive experience. It was even—figuratively speaking—a second life for Yorkie. We see those who are marginalized and devalued, get to live. It's a digital corrective for a tangible situation. Two people who loved one another, got to be together, no judgment.

There are a lot of religious themes as well in this episode. Not overtly, but it does refer to a digital afterlife, after all. No one really knows what happens after you die. People have their theories, but you won't truly "know" until it's your turn, if that makes sense. But in the future, to be absent from the body could mean that you are present in the cloud. Our life spans are so short, that it just doesn't seem fair. The best hack is this option, so it would seem.

Also of note was the time limit placed on the participants. They were allowed no more than five hours a week, and their participation in the simulation would end at exactly midnight. Really evokes that whole story of Cinderella, who had the chance to dress up lavishly and go to a ball—that is as long as she made it home before midnight. Because at that time, her carriage would turn into a pumpkin.

Kelly's husband Richard did not want to "stick" around in San Junipero. For the audience, he represented the traditional Christian view of wanting to return to God, and not believing in life ever after in the form of San Junipero. The notion of a digital afterlife must be a hard concept for those with traditional views to embrace. Factor in that they were both still grieving the loss of their daughter, and that she never got the opportunity, it's hard to blame Richard. The notions of sacrifice and long suffering are also heavy themes here.

For two characters that die, both Yorkie and Kelly also show surprising growth. Yorkie rejected the oppressive, religious outlook of her parents and their attitudes towards sexuality. Meanwhile, Kelly overcomes her grief and guilt about her husband and daughter's passing.

This special, Emmy Award-winning episode is about life, second chances, and a glimpse of hope for the possible future. This is part of the reason that this episode resonated with so many people, myself included. It's one of my favorites, and being the nerd that I am, I have tried to estimate how far into the future this *Black Mirror* episode could be.

The possibility of having a fully immersive, life like virtual reality system is still a ways off. So let's not talk about the tech, but the plausible timeline. Indulge my theory for a moment. Let's say Kelly is in her early 20's in 2002—the last year she visited in the simulation. In the end credits, the tombstone says that Kelly passed at 73 years old. If the eras that she chose to visit in San Junipero are adjacent with her life timeline, than that means this technology first emerged roughly sometime in the early 2050's. I could be wrong, but it's just a fan theory.

The unfortunate reality however, is that we live in an unjust world. People, for made up reasons or no reason at all, are robbed of the prospect of a decent life by illness, accidents, wars, and a myriad of other tragic occurrences. Reformers are talked down, and told that humane change would cost too much. Our society seems to have given up on making the physical world better, so many people retreat to virtual ones to fulfill their needs and desires.

San Junipero is just one of the possible, logical conclusions of our world now. If those who want to live on in a virtual world are allowed to experience the bliss they were denied in life, then that is one positive aspect of an emerging technology like virtual reality. We are told that life is like a game, and we have to play it right to win big. However, not everyone has the same stash of needed items in their inventory. Sometimes, life just abruptly unplugs us from the game. Given this non-virtual reality, what is so wrong about anyone taking the chance to push the button to continue?

Episode 5: Men Against Fire

Aired: October 21, 2016
Director: Jacob Verbruggen
Writer: Charlie Brooker
Cast: Malachi Kirby (as Stripe), Madeline Brewer (Raiman), Sarah Snook (Medina), Michael Kelly (Arquette), Kola Bokinni (Lennard), Loreece Harrison (Dream Girl), Francis Magee (Parn Heidekker)

"Humans. I mean.. we don't actually want to kill each other." - Arquette

One doesn't have to be a prophet to know that there will still be war in mankind's future. As technology advances, those leaps and bounds will be applied on the battlefield. "Men Against Fire" follows the combat experience of a newly enlisted soldier, Stripe. In the near future, a group of genetically deformed humans called "roaches" terrorize the rest of humanity. Stripe, as part of a team, is sent to liberate a village from an infestation.

These futuristic soldiers are equipped with a neural implant called the MASS system. Developed by the U.S. military, this implant allows for communication between soldiers, supplies all necessary intel, and even assists in their aim. There's even a metric indicating their accuracy percentage. Sounds like a video game, doesn't it? Unfortunately, the stakes here are of more consequence than a high score on the leaderboard.

On his first mission, after raiding a compound of a religious man, Stripe kills two roaches the man had been harboring. In the chaos, before they are shot, the roaches flash some sort of device, momentarily dazing Stripe and giving him a headache. As the unit returns to base, Stripe is regarded as a hero. Thinking his headache is caused by his implant, he checks in with the medics to report the malfunction. Uneasy with the whole experience, he meets with Arquette.

Arquette, the army doctor, congratulates Stripe on his battlefield exploits. He explains away Stripe's unease as normal, post-battle jitters, and recommends that he get some good rest. Apparently, the MASS implant can help with that too.

For successes on the battlefield, soldiers are rewarded with a vivid sexual encounter, provided of course by their implant as part of a dream sequence. Featuring the woman Stripe dreamed of the night before, the moment glitches out. But that's only the beginning of glitches.

The neural implant further malfunctions while in the field, as Stripe notices that his sense of smell was returning. Due to the terrible smell of roaches, the implant was supposed to cut off smell entirely, yet he could smell the grass.

On the second mission out since his implant began to malfunction, things began to unravel. Stripe and Raiman are sent on a search and neutralize mission to root out some roaches holed up in an abandoned housing complex. With Raiman as his cover, Stripe enters the complex ready to shoot anything that moves, but to his surprise, he sees a woman and child, hiding in fear for their lives. But all Raiman sees are two roaches and a struggle ensues.

Stripe realizes that his eyes have been lying to him as Caterina—the woman he saved from Raiman—tells him that the MASS system is distorting his view and making them see people as roaches. He learns that it's all part of an extermination that began 10 years after a war. Certain people were tracked, their DNA checked, and marked as genetically inferior to the rest of humanity. And to get the soldiers to play along, they were made to see them as monsters.

Once back in military custody, Stripe is told the unvarnished truth from Arquette. The MASS system was created to help soldiers be more efficient in the field, by desensitizing them to the realities of war. The implant blocks the smell of the blood, and the shrieks of those begging for their lives. Good soldiers don't need those getting in the way of their job.

War is more efficiently fought when you can dehumanize your enemy. When the people that you are pulling the trigger on are regarded as "the other" then killing them is easier. Arquette says: "They look just like us, that's why they are so dangerous." He explains that in military history, soldiers were often reluctant to fire upon the enemy. So they fixed that. The MASS system is literally a hack, a way of breaking the natural inclination of human beings to show mercy to one another.

Stripe, horrified by this, snaps and holds Arquette responsible for tricking him. Defending himself, Arquette turns off Stripe's eyes, blinding him. While he flails around the room, Arquette presents him with two choices. Either comply, and have his memories of this all erased, or be presented with a constant loop of everything he has done for the military, but this time uncensored. He would also be thrown in jail. Stripe agrees to have his memory wiped, and is discharged from the military.

Stripe goes "home" to a beautiful house and his dream girl, but in reality it's just a run down shack, and he's there by himself. A beautiful lie though is preferable to the ugly truth. Stripe took the blue pill, as most people would under those circumstances.

Episode 6: Hated in The Nation

Aired: October 21, 2016
Director: James Hawes
Writer: Charlie Brooker
Cast: Kelly Macdonald (Karen Parke), Faye Marsay (Blue Colson), Benedict Wong (Shaun Li), Jonas Karlsson (Rasmus Sjoberg), Joe Armstrong (Nick Shelton), Elizabeth Berrington (Jo Powers), Charles Babalola (Tusk)

"I didn't expect to find myself living in the future but here the fuck I well am."- Karen Parke

Sometimes, the solution to a problem creates more potential problems. "Hated In The Nation" is a crime drama about police working to solve a series of murders. The culprit isn't who or what you might expect however—they're robot bees.

Unlike the murder hornets that fortunately have not shown up as of this writing, these robot bees are a real and ever present threat for our heroes. In response to the extinction of real bees, a futuristic society responds by creating drones—or Autonomous Drone Insects(ADIs)—to replace their function.

The episode starts with the testimony of Karen

Parke, a detective chief inspector working on a high profile murder case that started in the Spring. Jo Powers, a controversial and widely despised journalist, was discovered at home with her throat slashed. In a flashback to May 15th, we see two important connections. Firstly, there is an online petition to have Powers fired for an insensitive hot take article about Gwen Marbury, a disabled activist who committed suicide. Secondly is a news story about the honeybee mimicking drones that have been in operation for the second summer in a row.

Jo Powers is scoffed at in public and even receives a cake with a special hateful message. Not bothered by this, she eats a slice and uncorks a bottle of wine to go along with it. Hateful comments is something she's quite used to, and even revels in. She checks Twitter to see a hashtag #DeathToJoPowers trending. Relishing in the public evisceration, Powers does not seem at all perturbed by the negative attention on or offline.

Another focal point is a rapper known as Tusk, who was ruthless in critiquing the TikTok style dancing video of one of his nine year-old fans. The kid wanted to be just like him, and Tusk just cuts him down while he's on a late night interview. That is a pretty heartless way to come at such a young kid.

Karen Park is called to the crime scene, and meets Blue Coulson, a digital forensics expert who is shadowing her on the case. Blue had previous worked on the Ian Rannoch case, which is a connection to a past episode. The lead investigator explains that Jo Powers is the victim and that they have their work cut out for them, because her last column provoked a lot of ire. Once they gain access to Powers apartment, they find her laid out with her throat slashed wide open. Blood is splattered on the walls. There were no signs of a forcible entry, and Twitter mentions were still coming in. The pair confiscate the remains of the uneaten cake as evidence, planning to track down who sent it to her.

The next day, while going over the CCTV tapes from outside of the home of Jo Powers, they find that no one came in or out. With that part of the investigation cold, they decide to speak with Powers' husband, who was stabbed and hospitalized. He tells them the gruesome story of how it happened. Seemingly, Jo Powers went into a seizure, banged her head against a desk, and cut her own throat. Horrified, but not totally buying his story, Karen next decides to investigate who sent the cake to her.

This leads to teacher Liza Bahar. Blue points out that Liza tweeted #DeathToJoPowers, and took part in sending the cake to the journalist. Liza, like many, says that it was just an online thing. For her, it was just an expression of her disdain. Liza doesn't even know who started the hashtag, merely hopping on the Twitter bandwagon. That's pretty on point as to how social media works.

Not being able to charge her with anything, Blue and Karen let Liza off with a warning. Further, they hear from the toxicology department that there was nothing in the cake that could have killed Jo Powers. As a result, the police have no choice but to bring her husband in for further questioning.

We next see that Tusk was another target of the #DeathTo hashtag. He was getting savaged online for being mean to one of his young fans. After one of his shows, Tusk steps outside to smoke, but starts yelling in pain, grabbing at his ear. Not knowing what was going on, his entourage rushed him to the hospital—but it was too late. During an MRI scan, the techs hear a pop. They find the remnants of one of the bee drones covered with blood, just near Tusks head.

And so the case was beginning to come together. Once Powers' autopsy was complete, Karen and Blue find out that an ADI was also involved in her demise. This one had burrowed its way into her brain, planting itself in the pain center. The pain was so intense, that Powers had cut her own throat just to make it stop. Damn.

Following this new lead, the two take a trip to Granular Headquarters, the company responsible for creating the ADIs. In the lobby, a gigantic G is made from a swarm of the robot bees. Blue takes a swat at them, causing the swarm to move before realigning itself back into the G formation. They are greeted by representatives of the company and pass a greenhouse full of plants being pollinated by the drone bees. There are some really good, and convincing metallic wing sound effects in this scene.

The ADIs were created because of the extinction of the honeybee, an extrapolation of what could actually happen in the future. Not only are the drones not piloted by anyone, but they're also solar powered and able to replicate themselves into a hive and print more of themselves, much like a 3D printer. So they can reproduce—how comforting.

During Karen and Blue's trip to Granular, they discover that one of the ADIs went offline the same evening Jo Powers was killed. After speaking with project lead Erasmus, they learn that in order for that to happen, someone had to gain access to a diagnostic controller. And what that meant was that either an employee, or former employee, of the company have hacked the robot bees. And these bees are all over the country. Talk about build up.

Once they return to police headquarters, Karen and Blue are greeted by Shaun Li, a National Crime Agency officer who was following the Tusk case. Blue notices that both Tusk and Powers were involved in online firestorms, including the #DeathTo hashtag. Further, he discovers that they were all started by bots, just to get the social media hate engine revved up. Blue explains to the team that it's being done with automated spam accounts.

And inside the avatar photos of the spam accounts, are little bees.

Attached to the spam links are videos showing instructions for the something called the Game of Consequences. The "game" involved choosing a person, posting their name and photo with the hashtag #DeathTo on Twitter, and whoever trends the highest, gets eliminated by 5:00 p.m. If tweets could kill, could be another name for this episode.

Finally with a solid lead, Blue scours the platform to figure out who the next target of this sick game would be. And it looks to be Clara Meades, who is trending after taking a photo that she is pretending to urinate on a war memorial. Wasting no time, the team tracks her location and rush to Clara's apartment in an attempt to save her life.

Karen contacts Clara ahead of time to let her know that she is in danger. Furthermore, they tell her to stay put until the police and the feds get there. Meanwhile, Blue contacts their contact at Granular HQ, to let him know to track any rogue robot bees that may pop up in the area. Erasmus tells them about a method of tracking down whoever is doing this.

The group rush to Clara's apartment just as there's a detection of a breach in one of the nearby ADI swarms. One bee goes offline. While they have Clara in custody, the bee appears on top of the complex's security camera. Fortunately they were able to successfully get her out and into a house that is away from the city. However, that bee had managed to crawl its way into the car, and waited until they got to the house to come out.

The police and FCA agent hide Clara upstairs with closed windows. Erasmus contacts Blue, telling her that he is not able to track the hacker. To make matters worse, while they were on the phone, his communication center told him that a swarm nearby the house had gone offline. They lost control of the entire swarm in seconds. Erasmus realizes that the hacker has control of all of the bees.

Shaun, who is downstairs, sees an entire swarm of bees headed to the house. Not able to call due to the hacker's interference, he sends them a text to exit the house. Blue and Karen escort Clara out, but aren't able to avoid the swarm and retreat back into the house to hide in the bathroom. In a terrifying scene, we see swarms of bees find their way into the house, crawl through the vents in the bathroom, and get to Clara. And all it takes is one.

One of the ADIs crawl up Clara's nose, burrows into her brain, and kills her right in front of Karen and

Blue. Once the mission is complete, the other bees in the house just stay there. It was an exercise in futility, to save her from a miniature assassin.

Afterwards, Blue and Karen go back to Erasmus at Granular HQ. They learn the robot bees have miniature cameras in them, and can use facial recognition software. The British government had been using the bees to conduct massive surveillance—something Shaun was not thrilled to have revealed. Government and the abuse of technology, what a surprise.

In an attempt to protect the next target, Shaun shows up at the office of Tom Pickering. They raise the idea of shutting down social media, but are shot down. Shaun shows the cabinet a live feed of soldiers in the field detonating a bomb near a hive of ADIs. At first they seem to be destroyed, but the bees just manage to reassemble, and attack the soldiers. The drones cannot be dealt with that easily.

The liaison group finally discover who is behind the hacking—Garrett Scholes. A former employee of Granular, Scholes has released a Unabomber-like manifesto talking about social media and its lack of accountability. His endgame here is to make people feel the consequences of what they say online.

In an attempt to shut the system down, they find Scholes using a geo-location tag in his photos. The only problem is that it was a set up. Scholes wanted the authorities to find his location and left a burned up hard drive with the schematics to the program. Karen, seeing this as a bit too good to be true, is hesitant on the idea of using this off switch to shut everything down.

At first it seemed that the bees were seemingly under the control of Granular again. That was until

Scholes's program finished working through the system, and took over total control. They now targeted 387,000 people—everyone who used the hashtag #DeathTo.

This was a really dark episode. It may seem like an understatement, but this slow building, crime drama had so many disturbing elements to it. The point, I believe, is to make us look at how vitriolic social media can be towards people under public scrutiny. Black Mirror fans immediately thought of this episode when we started hearing—thankfully fake—news reports about murder hornets. Anyway, looking at what our society is makes us flinch at what we say about people we have never met. Think of how often and how quickly a public figure can become the focal point of online ridicule. While we never really ask ourselves if it's right, most of us just go along with it.

This episode brings Season 3 to a close. Anyone who was worried about *Black Mirror* deviating from the formula of dark subjects due to a broader audience—and an early happy ending—had unfounded fears at that point.

Season 4

Episode 1: USS Callister

Aired: December 29, 2017
Director: Toby Haynes
Writer: Charlie Brooker
Cast: Jesse Plemons (Robert Daly), Cristin Milotti (Nanette Cole), Jimmi Simpson (Walton), Michaela Coel (Shania), Billy Magnussen (Valdack), Milanka Brooks (Elena Tulaska)

"Why won't you fight back?"- Nanette

It's said that we can be whomever we want on the internet. The nature of the net allows aspects of ourselves—that we normally hide—to come out. And it doesn't always mean that the person will play nicely with others. "USS Callister" begins focused on the inner life of Robert Daly, a game designer working at a huge future game company, Callister. Robert is the Chief Technical Officer of the company, and the designer of Infinity, an immersive space exploration game.

Despite his accomplishments however, Robert isn't respected at all in the company. James Walton, the head of the company, has open contempt for Robert. The employees who are junior in relation to Robert don't show him much regard. Even the receptionist barely looks up from her phone when interacting with him.

By all accounts, he is treated like a loser. While he is disregarded in his real life however, he would turn inwards toward the game he created, building a digital galaxy that revolved around him.

In his world, it's Captain Daly and he's in charge of the USS Callister of Space Fleet, a modded version of Infinity based on his favorite TV show that audiences should find reminiscent of *Star Trek.* Inside the game, Robert is unquestionably the man, thwarting the plots of villains, leading his crew out of dangerous situations, and earning the affections of his female shipmates. No harm in escapist fantasy, right? There's just one downside to this digital co-splay here—the other characters are not willing participants.

While Daly himself is real, the supporting characters in his game are actually digital representations of his co-workers. If you've watched the other episodes up until now, you'll know what it means that these representations are actually cookies captured by Robert. He obtained samples of their DNA from items in the office and used them to create characters for his perverse pleasure. While the real Robert is meek, Captain Daly is a tyrant and exceptionally harsh to his shipmates at the slightest provocation. The digital version of James is especially singled out for special abuse, as Robert acts out revenge fantasies.

This story is reminiscent of the *Twilight Zo*ne episode "Five Characters in Search of An Exit" where people who think they are real are trapped in a cylinder. The difference here though. is that when Robert adds a digital copy of Nanette to his compulsory game, it would eventually blow up his entire digital realm. The irony is, in the actual world, Nanette admired Robert's mind as we saw in the early part of the episode. Maybe if he had tried to get to know her instead, he could have had a real life fantasy.

Like many of her co-workers, new hire Nanette finds herself transported to a realm that she did not ask to be in. Upon her arrival, the others try to explain the situation gently, knowing full well Robert's sadistic nature. But she wants no part of the game. And once she was beamed back into the bridge, she got to learn that the hard way.

Seeing that she was not going to play along, Robert put his hand up in her direction and he snaps his fingers. Just like that her face disappears. She has no eyes, and no mouth, but her sensations tell her that she can't breathe. It's reminiscent of the scene in *The Matrix* where Agent Smith closed Neo's mouth so he couldn't talk on the phone. Nanette found herself on the floor, suffocating, with Robert refusing to give her face back until she agrees to submit to his authority as the captain. He also warns her that she will not die—you need his permission to die. After being sufficiently broken, Nanette relents. She gestures that she will submit, and Robert snaps his fingers again. Nanette is given back her face and she was ready to play along.

Their next mission depicts an encounter with Valdack and his giant space bug, Robert's chosen nemesis. During the encounter however, Robert gets a call for a pizza delivery and pauses the game, leaving his avatar in suspended animation. We see the real life Robert wake up out of his game-induced trance, take the device off of his temple, and answer the door.

While he is away, the others drop the co-splay act and start talking to each other normally. We learn that the big Starship Trooper type space bug is a copy of Jillian from accounting. Robert turned her into a giant roach for crossing him one too many times. Even Q would balk at this guy. Nanette spends the downtime looking at the device in Robert's hand. She's discouraged from trying anything by the others out of fear of brutal reprisal. She relents just as Robert returned. He then defeats Valdack by telling him there was a naked lady behind him, and shooting him in the back when he looks. Captain Benjamin Sisko, he is not. Who needs developed strategy when you are the unquestionable ruler of this closed off universe?

And with Valdack vanquished, the team begins to act out their relief at being saved by their wise captain. Back on the bridge, and just like the opening sequence, Robert has this post mission ritual of kissing his female shipmates. Shania and Elena comply, but Nanette is not having it. When Robert grabs her, she pushes him away and smacks him. It must hurt to get rejected by a digital copy of a person. However, he decides to show mercy on Nanette and forewarns her that next time he may not feel so benevolent. Then he exits the game.

What sends Nanette over the edge is what she finds out afterwards. Apparently, the copies that he has created of his co-workers don't have any genitalia. It's a wholesome universe, which reflects the mods stunted personal development. She talks to Kabir, asking him about the device Robert brings with him. He explains that it is an omnicorder, which is a connection between the game and the outside world. Since it is actually a game, Nanette figures out how to send an invite to her real world self, with a message asking for help. Unfortunately, it materialized as a text invite from Robert Daly.

In the real world, Nanette approaches Robert to ask him if he sent her a game invite to Infinity. He says no, but has already figured out what they tried to do. Plausibly, he told the real Nanette that it was just spam, and to update her security settings. Also telling, is that at no point did we see the real life Robert get Nanette's number. He logs back into the game, ready to exact his wrath.

Robert goes on this rant about the virtues of Space Fleet, and the purpose of it. According to his twisted outlook, these digital programs are messing it all up. Seeing that he is livid, Nanette cops to sending out the message. He casts his hand up, ready to punish her, but not before Shania jumps in front of her, pleading that she's new and doesn't understand. He at first seemingly relents, but turns Shania into one of those giant space bugs and has the crew drop her off on some abandoned planet. He leaves Nanette in the game by herself overnight to think about what just happened.

Nanette finds herself in tears, staring out the window of the USS Callister. But there was hope. She notices a wormhole and surmises that would be their ticket out of there. The wormhole in actuality was the Christmas update patch for Infinity that was currently in the works. While Robert's space fleet mod was sectioned off from the rest of the game, this wormhole represented the rest of Infinity. In order for them to escape, Nanette wanted to fly into the wormhole, even if it meant that they ceased to exist as coded versions of human beings. Better to be nothing, than trapped in a hell. Everyone was onboard with the plan, except James.

Originally, Robert's space fleet mod was just him and James, and he had done everything he could to break him. What finally worked however, was using his son—or a copy of him to be accurate. One day when the real life James brought his son into work, Robert used the opportunity to digitally clone a version of the six-year-old Tommy by stealing his DNA from a lollypop left around the office.

With his son in the game, Robert was able to truly torture James. He threw the digital version of Tommy out of an airlock and made James watch. James doesn't want to ever step out of line, because he knows that Robert still has all of their DNA in a fridge in his kitchen. Therefore, even if they "die" he can bring them right back whenever he feels like it. What a freaking conundrum. But Nanette has a plan to get the lollypop, as well as the other items.

By blackmailing the real Nanette, using compromising photos of her that digital Nanette has access to, they manage to rope her in to helping them. Inside the game, she volunteers to go on a mission alone with Robert and distracts him. Stripping down, she entices him to join her in the digital ocean. Meanwhile, the team clones a version of Robert's omnicorder, and uses it to order a pizza. And this time, when he pauses the game to answer the door, Nanette makes a run for it to join back with the rest of the crew.

Back in the real world, while Robert answers the door, the real life Nanette breaks into his apartment and grabs the items with his coworkers DNA from the fridge. Also, she switches the connection piece that Robert puts on his temple with a dud disc, to further stall him from logging back in. Robert doesn't even tip the pizza man, showing that his jerkiness is seeping into his real life, and when he logs back into the game, he sees that Nanette is not there. He quickly finds out they are making their attempt at an escape, and pursues them in a smaller ship.

In the most *Star Trekish* moment of the episode, the crew discovers that there is not enough time to chart a safe course to the wormhole. Instead, they have to go through a field of asteroids—and if they don't make it, they will be stuck there forever. Unfortunately, they hit a big asteroid on the final swerve of the ship, knocking out their engine. And the only way to restart it, is to do it manually. James volunteers, even knowing that it will delete him. But before he does, he has one last conversation with Robert. He tells him that he should have appreciated him more in the real world, but then he reminds him about his son and throws the switch to restart the engine. The digital James Walton is incinerated, sacrificing himself so the others can escape.

They make it to through the wormhole successfully, looking forward to being deleted. And yet, something stranger happens. When they come through on the other side, they are still alive and in one piece. They are wearing updated space suits, a new bridge, and in the official version of the game. Robert's Space Fleet build was deleted by the game's firewall. This also means that his controls were disabled. Everyone was made whole and in a brief moment, we see Nate check to see if his package is there. He is relieved that it is, and shoots a look at Shania. Hilarious. Robert, on the other hand, ends up stuck in his computer, while his real self goes into a comatose like state.

This episode is a commentary on the modern nature of show fandom, and an illustration on what some scholars refer to as the online dis-inhibition effect. Technology emboldens some, as anyone can see from many message boards and social media sites—anonymity and distance turns some into keyboard killers, ready with clap back and all kinds of insults. Think of how abusive some traditional *Star Wars* fans have been towards some of the actors of the new trilogy. Fan bases that are territorial and protective of their favorite series have, at times, shown themselves to be hostile to any perceived deviations. There are times when we see that it is clearly not about canon, but the people in the roles themselves. Consider for example, the vitriol directed at Kelly Marie Tran on Instagram.

Robert Daly is the personification of a quietly resentful, but hate filled "nice guy"—quotation marks emphasized. If we think of these copies of his co-workers as sentient life, then they have the right to not be tortured and terrorized. And it makes him a monster. There is a chasm between the idealism that Robert espouses, and wraps himself with in his Space Fleet mod, while at the same time being an insufferable tyrant where it is safe for him to do so.

Nanette on the other hand is the opposite of Robert and emerges as a leader to steer the crew out of captivity. Just as clever as him, but a lot more moral. Technology can enable petty tyrants, or be utilized as a force to free people. USS Callister shows that it can go either way—it just depends who is in the captain's chair.

The Binge Watcher's Guide to Black Mirror

This episode is one of the most visually impressive expressions of the series as well. As a fan of *Star Trek*, this was a really good nod to the ethos of the series, and stood out to me as one of the brightest lights of season four. When I first saw the poster for USS Callister, I was sold. Michaela Cole's character Shania Lowry is basically a nod to Uhura from the original Star *Trek*.

Another point that can be made about Robert's inadequate coping skills, is that if Robert had pivoted a little bit in his real life, and found ways to stand up for himself, he would not have wound up in the predicament that he ended up in. But no, that would have been way too hard for him to do. He used his "smarts" to access ways of torturing copies of people, instead of using them to find a better way to navigate his real life. It was a fitting punishment that he ends up with his consciousness stuck inside his own computer.

We don't see it in the episode, but it is somewhat implied that Robert was going to die. Some would ask, is this too harsh of a punishment? But then you think about the fact that he killed a copy of a child. So, no. The type of person who gets their jollies through torturing people is a horrible person regardless. Just because you can be a prick in the digital realm, doesn't mean that you should. When he put more focus on building an entire bubble universe, but chose not to engage the real world in a better way, he hacked himself out of a more fulfilled existence. It is the story of Tron, but he is the evil administrator.

The episode ends with yet another supposed Billy badass character crossing paths with Nanette. Gamer691, voiced by Aaron Paul—who played Jesse Pinkman from

Breaking Bad—shows up to trade. After finding out that the USS Callister has nothing to trade, he tells them to get out of his quadrant or get blasted. Not wanting to risk a fight after leading her crew through a dangerous wormhole, Nanette decides to hit the warp drive. This is sort of a mirror to what Robert was—a person who wants to be the domain master of something that really didn't matter. Jesse Plemons was also in *Breaking Bad*, as a character who had a role in tormenting Jesse Pinkman. That connection didn't miss me either.

Robert is not the last person that we will see who loses his life over the mistreatment of sentient, digital life. Play stupid games, win stupid prizes.

Episode 2: Arkangel

Aired: December 29, 2017
Director: Jodie Foster
Writer: Charlie Brooker
Cast: Rosemarie Dewitt (As Marie), Brenda Harding (Sara), Owen Teague (Trick)

Helicopter parenting mode activated. In a dangerous world, parents go to extreme lengths to protect their children. Rightfully so, but how far is too far? Marie, a single mother, would find out the hard way in "Arkangel."

Marie quite naturally freaks out when she loses track of her pre-school daughter Sara while out at a park. And instead of being more aware of her surroundings, Marie embraces a technological solution. Soon after the park incident, she takes three year-old Sara to the office of Arkangel, a company that provides a service to protect children. After explaining that this technology has been tested, and that it is safe, the representative has Sara watch cartoons while they implant a device into her. Afterwards, Marie is provided with a tablet device referred to as a parental hub that tracks Sara's location, her heart rate, other vitals, and what she is seeing in real time. There is even a feature to adjust what Sara is seeing, and filter it out if it is too stressful for her. Sort of a *Black Mirror* version of parental control.

The representative demonstrates the effectiveness of the implant by showing footage of a soldier shooting a gun. Of course, this footage was from the "Men Against Fire" episode, which is not at all a coincidence. Like how the military implant distorted what the soldiers saw, the Arkangel implant does the same for children. The person shooting the gun is pixelated, and the sound garbled.

Marie's father, however, was skeptical of this program from the beginning. He espoused the idea that children need some sort of latitude to be. Marie retorts that her arm was broken as a child because her father didn't put in a baby gate, and she wants to spare Sara of some of the unpleasant experiences that she has gone through.

On an outing with her daughter, Marie activates the filter on Sara's eyes. Normally, their neighbor's barking dog is a source of anxiety for her, but when they walk by now, all Sara sees is the dog's pixelated outline. Unfortunately, there would be downsides to the filter. The next day, Marie goes to work and leaves Sara with her grandfather. While they were painting, granddad has a stroke and collapses on the floor. But because this is a stressful situation, he becomes pixelated and Sara is unable to hear her grandfather ask her to go phone for help. Fortunately, the tablet also tracks cortisol increases in Sara, and went off while Marie was in her office. Her father survives, but is must walk with a cane.

The story fast forwards a few years, and her grandfather passes away. Marie, of course is at the funeral, but the parental feature pixelates her face because she is crying. Anything that can stress out Sara is blocked, meaning that her emotional growth is bound to be stunted. Sara is nine and doesn't even know what blood is. In school, she has to have other kids describe things to her. Even a simple thing like choosing which color to make a character's hair, she needs to ask her mother about. The other kids are aware that she has the neural implant in her brain, which results in her being ostracized and excluded. She's regarded as a walking surveillance camera.

Being unable to fully see and experience everything that her peers are able to begins to wear on Sara. When at home, she tries to draw an image from a video that she could not see herself, but had described to her. Even that, she could not do—the implant blurred out the image of blood as soon as she drew it. Frustrated, and likely numb, Sara pricks herself with a pencil. She wants to see blood, but even her own is pixelated. Marie sees the notification on her tablet go off, and rushes to finds out what is happening upstairs. Marie tries to stop Sara from hurting herself, but gets slapped. The acting out has begun.

The next scene is a trip to the child psychologist. In these scenes, Sara is shown images of people and what they are doing. It becomes increasingly clear that she is not emotionally adept at figuring out cues, or emotional states, because the Arkangel system blocked everything deemed "bad" in her life. In speaking to the child psychiatrist, Marie inquires if Sara was autistic. The doctor said that she was not, and that it was more so a case of Sara rebelling against the parental monitoring system that is being used to raise her. She was denied many experiences and feels resentful of her mom's tight control over her.

It's then that Marie realizes that she did this to her daughter. The Arkangel system, which was a free trial, never did actually launch nationwide. For ethical reasons, it was banned in Europe and soon to be pulled in the United States as well. On top of that, the neural implant can't be removed. There's no clicking to undo on that. What the psychiatrist recommends is to turn off the filter, and throw the parental hub tablet away. Of course Marie doesn't do that, or the episode would be over too quick. What she does instead is turn the system off, and shelf the tablet.

Now, Sara has to suddenly adjust to life without Arkangel. No fuzzy pictures, or a second set of eyes looking. It's here, when she starts to get up to speed on all the things she was denied. Trick, one of her classmates, shows her videos of porn, viral YouTube videos of fights, beheadings, and all of that. It was like a crash course in the grim parts of reality. After living a life with her mom literally being able to see her every move, Sara gradually acclimates to school as a normal adolescent. Surprisingly. Marie leaves the child tracking tablet in a box in the attic.

A few years pass by, and Sara is a teenager now. She even has a set of friends, including Trick, who's older and into somewhat shady business. Sara is looking for an opportunity to hang out with him, but knows that if she asks her mom, the answer will be a flat out no. Using an all girl's movie night at a friend's house for a cover story, Sara meets up with Trick instead.

It's past 11:00, and he is offering her puffs of weed, while Marie is back home, a bit concerned.

The Binge Watcher's Guide to Black Mirror

Sara's phone is going straight to voicemail. She called the house that was allegedly being used for the movie night, and was told she wasn't there. As a last resort, Marie rushes upstairs to the attic, digs the parental hub tablet out of the box, and plugs it in. She turns the optic feed on to see Sara's view of Trick on top of her. Horrified, Marie turns the feed off.

Marie waits for Sara to come home, and even though she knows about where she really was, she doesn't confront Sara right then and there. The next day, Sara tells her mom that she is going to be home late from school. Of course, she is really going to see Trick again. We find out that Trick is not just into dealing weed, but that he is also moving coke. Sara asks him for some and he obliges. Meanwhile, Marie finds out because she has the tablet back up and running and it sent her a notification that her daughter's heart rate was up.

At this point, Marie is beside herself. She uses the timeline feature of the tablet to run everything back, and get a still shot of Trick's face. She then uses a facial recognition website to find out who this guy is, where he works, and the next day confronts him in person. She warns Ryan (Trick) to stay away from her daughter, because not only does she know that he is older than her, but she also knows he is selling drugs. She threatens that if he doesn't stay away from Sara, she will go to the cops. Totally spooked, he agrees to leave Sara the hell alone.

Now Trick is ghosting Sara, and she doesn't know why. When she confronts him at his job, Trick tells her that the whole situation was a mistake. Fully aware of the fact that Marie has the system on and can see him, he tells Sara that he doesn't want her anymore. Being a small built, dope peddling statutory rapist wouldn't work out too well for him if he were to get locked up after all. And Sara ends up hurt, confused, and still unaware of her mother's role in all of this. It's about to get even deeper.

The parental hub tablet sends a notification, and we see Marie headed to the pharmacy—the system has told her that Sara is pregnant. The following morning, Marie is crushing up morning after pills, to put in Sara's morning smoothie. She goes off to school, but begins to feel sick during class and ends up throwing up in the bathroom. Worse, when she visits the school nurse, she discovers it was an early contraception pill that made her sick—one she never took.

Sara comes home from school, and dumps the trash, finding the empty EC box. Furious, she storms upstairs to her mom's room and searches for the tablet. She finds it, and turns it on. Sara sees that it has the timeline of recent events, including footage of her sleeping with Trick. Mortified, she runs to her room, and starts pulling clothes out of her drawers—she's planning to run away. But she doesn't make it far however, because her mom comes back just in time.

When Marie gets upstairs, she finds the tablet on the floor. Turning it on, she sees herself looking at the tablet with her back turned. Sara is right behind her. She accuses her mom of watching her and grabs for the tablet. Managing to get it out of her hands, she tries to turn it off. It was then that Marie chooses to try and explain why she did what she did. She said that she was only trying to protect her, but Sara was not hearing it at all. They get into a fight where Sara ends up hitting Marie in the face with the tablet until she falls unconscious. The screen cracks, and the device is inoperable. Sara takes her duffle bag and gets out of the house.

When Marie comes to, Sara is long gone. Marie, all bloodied up, picks up the cracked tablet and walks just outside her home, screaming for Sara. The episode ends the way it began, with Sara lost to her.

Marie flashes back in her mind to the day her daughter was born, cycles through her pre-school years, school aged times, and finally to her as a teenager. What she doesn't realize is that through her actions, she has lost her daughter for good. Seeing that she would never have privacy while she is with her mom, Sara felt like she had no other choice than to run away from home.

Because of Marie clamping down so much, and putting too many guardrails on Sara, she hampered her personal development and stunted her growth. There were no counterbalances—it was either Marie's way, or the highway. In a highly symbolic ending, the story ends with a teenage Sara hitchhiking on a truck. She chose the literal highway.

What was supposed to help be the guardian over her life, was what ultimately motivated Sara to get away from her mother's controlling ways. It was a sad ending, but the true beginning of her life. What was meant to protect, ended up stifling.

As parents grapple with the realities of technology and how it can affect what it means to be a watchful guardian, there has to be a healthy balance. This episode was overprotective parenting to the 1000th power. There was a lot of sneaking around, and not even one conversation about Sara's behavior. The lesson here I believe, is to use technology as a tool, but not let it raise your child. Parent post alert.

Episode 3: Crocodile

Aired: December 29th, 2017
Director: John Hillcoat
Writer: Charlie Brooker
Cast: Andrea Riseborough (As Mia Nolan), Andrew Gower (Rob), Kiran Sonia Sawar (Shazia Akhand), Anthony Welsh (Anan Akhand)

Never underestimate how far someone will go to protect their livelihood. Mia is a successful executive with a dark past that comes back to bite her in "Crocodile." Responsible for the death of a cyclist over a decade ago, she and her business partner decide to get rid of the evidence, and never speak of the incident again.

That would change however, when Rob—years later—would come to Mia wrought with guilt over the incident. Mia, who had become a successful architect, becomes concerned with his guilt. Their argument as to whether he should come clean ends in Mia murdering him, to protect herself. Now that's two.

There is just one problem for Mia—she's becomes the subject of an investigation. Ironically, not directly though. Shazia, who is looking into an accident as an insurance investigator, is piecing together a case about a pedestrian hit by a pizza delivery van. She works for a company called Realm Insurance, and logs people's memories as part of claims. Using a device that connects to the side of your temple, she can retrieve and display memories for the time in question. The same night that Mia had killed Rob, a driver-less pizza delivery van hit a man. Mia had been looking out the window at the time, and witnessed it.

Shazia first takes the memory log of the man who was hit by the pizza van. Placing a green memory cube to the side of the guy's temple, she uses a gray box to witness the recollections. It shows him going into a comic book shop just before the accident, and the face of a woman in a yellow coat walking towards him on the street. While attempting to cross the street, he's hit by the van. It doesn't look like he was paying attention. Unable to gather any more info from him, Shazia decides to find the woman in yellow.

Using facial recognition software, Shazia tracks down her next witness, Noni. Showing up at Noni's, she gets her account, but Noni didn't actually witness the van hit the guy. She only turned around and saw him holding his arm in the middle of the snowy street. What she did notice though, was a flash from a camera. This leads to William, a dentist who was staying in the hotel that night. He was the man Mia saw in the building across from her.

Shazia hooks William up to the memory-mining machine and watches the dentist take a photo of a guy walking near his window naked. He tries to take another photo, but notices a woman in the window staring at what happened downstairs. And that woman was Mia.

Speaking to Farshad, the hotel receptionist, she wants to know who stayed in the room on the evening in question. Farshad can't give her much information, as Shazia is not with the police, but he does tell her that the guest watched a film that evening, and the choice stood out.

Shazia has to use her own investigative resources to find her next person. At this point, no one she has logged memories from, had actually witnessed the van hit him. She has an image of the woman in the window, but it's fuzzy. However, zooming in on the photo and plugging it into facial recognition software, it comes back with a match—Mia Nolan. It also comes up with her location. And so we're back to where we started. Shazia visits Mia at her home to log in her memories about the evening of the accident. Mia just wants to tell her that she saw the guy get hit, but does not want to be hooked up to the memory machine, afraid that the truth of her murder might come out with it. Shazia explains that legally, she has to report it if she was a witness to the accident, to which Mia grudgingly concedes. Mia excuses herself, and starts practicing her story in the bathroom.

While the memory playback machine does its work, Shazia sees the impact of the pizza van, and a whole lot more—it shows Rob dead on the floor, bleeding from the nose, and even the biker that they killed 15 years ago. She abruptly closes the memory box, saying that she has everything she needs. She tries to leave, but Mia follows her to her car. With the car engine stalled, Mia takes this advantage to smash the left side car window, and drag her out of the car.

We next see Shazia with her mouth gagged, tied up in some shed on Mia's property. Mia is deliberating as to whether or not she has to kill her too. Shazia tells her that she didn't tell anyone she was coming to Mia's house—something she is saying to protect her husband and child. Mia, unconvinced, connects Shazia to her memory machine. Their dynamic reversed, Mia sees an image of Anan, Shazia's husband. There's a tear coming from her eye, because Mia now knows what she has to do. In a shot outside the shed, we hear Mia beating Shazia to death with a wooden log. She then drives to Shazia's house, looking for her husband.

Mia breaks into the house, wearing a face mask and carrying a hammer. She first sees Anan in his living room, watching television, but doesn't attack. No, she waits for Anan to go upstairs to take a bath, before smashing him in the head with the hammer. He slides into the bathtub, dead, and Mia covers his body with the green towel. Thinking she's done, she tries to get out of the house, but Anan and Shazia's child sees her. It is not shown on screen, but it is implied that Mia kills the baby too. All done in time to make it to her son's play at 7:30 p.m.

The police have come to the house now and find Anan's body upstairs, as well as the baby. The baby had been born blind—Mia had killed a blind child. The police are aghast at this, and the only possible lead they have, is to connect the hamster in the child's room to the memory machine for clues. And it works.

It's the end of the play and we see Mia nervously clapping as the police pull up outside. She's busted and likely to get a whole bunch of time. Not only for the four people that she killed herself, but also for the role she played in covering up the death of the cyclist 15 years ago. At the very least, she was complicit in his murder.

The Binge Watcher's Guide to Black Mirror

"Crocodile" is like a futuristic "To Catch A Killer" type episode. In seeing the workings of the memory-mining machine, it is way more thorough than any lie detector test. If your own memories aren't private, then there's no way that you can hide what you have done. It's possible to mis-remember details, but is it possible to create a fabricated visual image to accompany them? You can leave details out, but your visual recollection will just fill them in.

Throughout the episode, we see Mia kill repeatedly to preserve the life she has built for herself. Crocodile is named such, because it is indicative of the tears that Mia cries before ending the life of her victims. She is not crying for them—she is crying for herself. As we know, crocodiles don't really cry. They just appear to do so. This is another one of those dark, twisted episodes that *Black Mirror* is known for.

Episode 4: Hang The DJ

Aired: December 29th, 2017
Director: Timothy Van Patten
Writer: Charlie Brooker
Cast: Georgina Campbell (As Amy) Joe Cole (Frank)

Love is hard to find, at least so it's said. These days people use dating apps to connect and find those they could be compatible with, but in the future, this could go a bit further. Do relationships have an expiration date? "Hang The DJ" challenges this idea.

Amy and Frank live in a world where couples are initially matched by a digital dating coach. The twist? Each relationship has an expiry date. The purpose—so it's explained—is to find the most compatible people, by gathering a large enough sample size. Following them on their first date, we see it even picked their meals. That's a good way to cut down on indecision.

Both tap their device at the same time, agreeing to see what the expiry date on their relationship will be. This time, it's only 12 hours. A single night. The two get in a driverless car and are driven to a small motel. They end up not having sex that night, and only hold hands.

Afterwards, both Amy and Frank ask the system why the interaction was so short. The system answers by noting that brief interactions can yield important data. Data on personal interactions, that is deep. What is really bugged out though, is that all relationships that are entered into must expire. And it appears to be compulsory, going by the security guards posted at the restaurant. They are told the system has a 99.8 percent accuracy rate.

Amy is immediately paired with a new guy, Lenny. Lenny is built in comparison to Frank, and they're paired for nine months. Frank meanwhile, is paired off with Nicola, who isn't exactly jumping with joy to be linked with him for a year. She's ill-tempered and snippy towards him, as if to say "Let's just get this over with." It's going to be a long year for Frank.

Amy, in contrast, is having a much better time with Lenny. The system has it set up where you tap the circular tablet to give your sexual consent, which Amy does without hesitation. Lenny, with this being his fifth date, is very experienced by this point. She finds that out then and there, and is having a great night. While Frank, on the other hand, not so much. He consented with Nicola, but it's not going well. He's not giving it to her the way she needs, and she has to instruct him. She basically said his stroke game was boring. Ouch.

After Nicola falls asleep, Frank looks at the tablet with the expiry date. He did it in the same manner in which people check their phones—with a blank look on his face that says "I gotta put up with her for a year?" Which is the case, and it's what the system recommends—or demands. Frank has to let the relationship play out, running down the time like a prison sentence.

When Frank and Amy bump into one another at a gathering, it's really obvious that they miss one another. Frank literally gets choked up, at least over the spinach garlic dip. Amy saves him, and they share a quick moment together before Lenny comes over. What could have been awkward, winds up being a conversation with no confrontation. No reason for shows of jealousy when the computer set everything up, I guess.

While Amy is getting what she needs from Lenny, some of his quirks begin to annoy her. The sound he makes after he takes a sip of water, the way he picks his ears—yikes. Nine months, and they have to live together. So do Frank and Nicola. Of course, Amy's second relationship ends before Frank's. Afterwards, the system sets Amy up with a string of 36 hour flings with different dudes. Frank on the other hand, has to run down the clock for the next three months with Nicola. It's like a sitcom situation, except it ain't funny. When the relationship ends, and they have to part ways, Nicola just walks off, ignoring him completely.

Frank goes on another date, and is surprisingly paired back again with Amy. She too is pleasantly surprised, and doesn't want to check the expiry date. She has been in so many different relationships, she mentions that she was beginning to dissociate. They both agree not to check it, and just enjoy each other's company for as long as they could.

And they have a great time reconnecting, and make sure not to waste the opportunities they missed the last time. Here they are, back together again, just letting things be natural—at least as much as possible, considering that they were re-matched by the system. But of course, as the time goes by, Frank became too curious and could not leave well enough alone. Late one night while Amy is asleep, he checks the system to see what the expiry date was. The system specifically warns that both participants must check it at the same time. In spite of that, Frank taps the circle tablet anyway to see how long he and Amy will be together. It comes up with five years. At least at first.

He is relieved, until the system starts re-calibrating the expiry date all on its own. The tablet continuously re-calibrates downwards, shaving more and more time off of their relationship. He begs for the system to stop, but it's automated and can't do that. It's a Hal 9000 moment, but for his love life. When the final re-calibration finishes, it's knocked down his time with Amy from five years, to 20 hours. Distraught, Frank realizes that he's made a big mistake.

The next day, Amy realizes that something is up. Frank, at first, does not tell her that he looked at the system. They try to go along as normal, but Amy senses that things are off. While out on a date, Frank admits that he looked at the system, and Amy understandably feels betrayed. They have their first big argument, and Amy walks away from Frank. She was angry with him for messing up something good.

After all of that, they were back out there on the scene. And this time, it was Franks fault. Amy feels disconnected with her next partner, and so does Frank. So much so that he was thinking of her, while with his new date. That's gotta blow. After a painful, system forced break up, they are each given a day for their ultimate pairing. Before that day however, they have the opportunity to meet someone of their choosing, to help with closure. And they immediately choose each other.

When they meet back up, Amy and Frank feel like it's a test, and that they have to rebel together. They have to escape over the wall and be with one another. They're stopped by security, with one of the guards pulling out their taser. But when she puts her hand over it, the guy freezes. Also, everyone around them does as well. This was a simulation. Of course it was.

What is really trippy about it all, is that this simulation was run 1000 times. Once they climb over the wall, Amy and Frank de-materialize into code, and we see all the different versions of themselves coupled. Of the thousand simulated dates, 998 rebellions were logged. Which lead to the 99.8 percent accuracy rate.

At the end of the episode, we see the real life Amy walk into a bar to meet the real life Frank. She pulls out her phone, and he does the same—a 99.8 percent match. This entire episode took place within the confines of a futuristic phone app. What a trip. Match.com better take notes or something.

What's really fascinating though, is how they deal with the idea of compatibility. Would we really want an app to pick who we are going to be with? Are humans that disconnected, that we don't want to go through the messiness of approaching, talking, and understanding one another's interests before a serious commitment?

In our society today, people really have a difficult time meeting their soulmate. As human relations get more distant, this is a positive example of how technology can help reconnect us. And it's only a matter of time before some company tries to take the guesswork out of the courting game. "Hang the DJ" is an upbeat episode, with a lot of philosophical thoughts about love, commitment, and relationships. I like how it's depicted that there is a bit of rebellion in every relationship. The varying ideas of what it means to settle as expressed by Amy were also interesting.

Perhaps, deferring to an app is the intelligent thing to do. Given that some online algorithms can predict human behavior, it might make sense to let our technology help us. That way, we'll see a lot less "it's complicated" relationship statuses, and more happy couples.

Episode 5: Metalhead

Aired: December 29, 2017
Director: David Slade
Writer: Charlie Brooker
Cast: Maxine Peake (Bella), Jake Davies (Clarke), Clint Dyer (Anthony)

Imagine being chased down by a murderous, robot dog. In what is arguably the most terrifying episode of the season, "Metalhead" is a cross between *The Terminator* and *Cujo*—a literal example of the dogs of war. Interestingly, this is the only episode of *Black Mirror* that was filmed entirely in black and white.

Three would be looters—Bella, Clarke and Anthony—are on a mission to secure goods from an abandoned warehouse. Bella had promised her sister that she would do all she can to secure what they needed. So all we know at that point, is that it's for a dying child.

While on the way to the warehouse, they noted that the pigs were all gone, and that the dogs had gotten rid of them. And everywhere they drive looked abandoned, as if people have had to flee due to some disaster.

Arriving at the warehouse, they finally find the box they were looking for, but in true horror movie fashion, a little, black metal dog is right behind it. The

Metalhead activates, spraying shrapnel into the air. The viewer is led to believe that the shrapnel itself is a weapon, but in reality they are trackers that bore into the skin. And just like that, the hunt is on.

They panic, drop the box, and make a run for it. But not before the dog shoots Anthony, killing him. Yes, the robot dog has a gun. It's *Black Mirror* after all. Bella escapes, driving away from the warehouse. Clarke, seeing that things have gone wrong, pulls off too. In the mayhem, there was no time to retrieve the box that Anthony now died for.

The dog, not at all finished, pursues Clarke. Metalhead runs, crashes through the back window door of the van, and effortlessly kills Clarke. Then, using some kind of prong device to take control of the steering, the dog continues to chase down Bella and almost runs her off of the road. What bought her time was that she had to drive the car off the path into a forest, and almost off of a cliff. The dog pursues, but Bella manages to escape before the car goes off the cliff with the dog in it.

But that wasn't enough. Bella escapes to an abandoned house, where she attempts to hole up and hide. It's a futile effort however, as the dog manages to track her the entire way. While Bella ends up finally killing the thing with a blast from a shotgun, it manages to shoot off a payload of additional trackers that bury into her skin. And she knows there will be more dogs coming for her now. Realizing this, Bella uses the radio one last time to say goodbye to her family, before taking a knife to her throat.

The episode ends with a group of robot dogs advancing to where Bella was. She never had a chance.

Back at the warehouse, still lying in the middle of the floor, was a box of teddy bears. The mission that cost them their lives was to get a teddy bear to comfort a dying child. And they were killed for it. This is one of the darkest more disturbing episodes, and the message might not be apparent upon viewing it.

What we see here is a spin on a concept that science fiction fans have been familiarized with since *Terminator*. The idea of a machine that hunts and kills humans is nothing new, but it does make me think of why, and what happened to get to this point. Why did the dogs kill the pigs? Was it some malfunction? This episode could be a commentary on the arbitrary and cruel nature of drone warfare.

With the U.S. Air Force now beginning to use robot dogs as part of their battle exercises, this episode predicts a bit too much. With the amount of resources that are poured into the military, the further development of such deadly, automated weaponry is pretty plausible. And with the cooperation of large companies, who is to say that it will stop there? Microsoft is already providing cloud computing services for the government. And much like how the military sends its spare gear to police departments, why wouldn't a company utilize such technology to guard warehouse inventory? *Black Mirror*, once again, shows us a plausible dystopia.

Episode 6: Black Museum

Aired: December 29, 2017
Director: Colm McCarthy
Writer: Charlie Brooker
Cast: Douglas Hodge (Rollo Haynes), Letitia Wright (Nish), Daniel Alpine (Dr. Peter Dawson), Aldus Hodge (Jack), Alexandra Roach (Carrie), Babes Olusanmokun (Clayton Leigh), Yasha Jackson (Emily), Amanda Warren (Angelica)

"How long can happiness realistically last anyhow?"
– Rolo Haynes

A museum is a collection of relics from the past and can show us how far a society has come, or perhaps a history that society is still yet to reckon with. They're a focal point for class trips, instructive to both teachers and students alike. So, imagine how much you can learn from a museum of the future? This is exactly what curator Rolo Haynes shows us in "Black Museum"—a collection curated by Mr. Haynes himself.

The owner of the Black Museum gets a visit from Nish, who is stopping by the town to visit her father. Rolo, a former medical technician consultant, originally opened the museum based upon his own career. Using the objects in the museum as a catalyst, he tells Nish three interrelated stories, about the dangers of technology.

This final episode of the fourth season is full of Easter eggs from previous seasons. We see the mask and shotgun of the hunter from "White Bear," the touch pad from "Arkangel," and other items that fans will recognize. You might consider the title to mean a *Black Mirror* museum. Even the structure of the episode is reminiscent of "White Christmas." If you have watched each season in order, it might be difficult to hold in your exclamations as you see the different artifacts. References to episodes from Season 1 are sprinkled throughout this hour-plus long tour of future tech. And all of this as Rolo weaves in and out of storytelling, showing his own culpability in all of the devices that he discusses.

Nish asks about one of the devices, a hairnet-like thing with blue bulbs all over it. And so Rolo begins to tell her the story of Dr. Peter Dawson, who worked at the emergency room of St. Junipers hospital in downtown New York City. As a doctor dedicated to saving the lives of his patients, he was struggling with the realities of mortality rates, due in part to them being unable to properly explain what was wrong with them.

Sympathetic—and looking to sell a product—Rolo presents Dr. Dawson with a solution, if not an ethically questionable one. What if there was a way to feel the pain of the patients, to help properly diagnose and treat them? Rolo Haynes, propositions the good doctor with precisely such a device. He shows him two dead lab rats, both with a device on their head. Rolo explains that one is a transmitter, and the other the receiver. At some time in the future, scientists had figured out how to transfer the memories, and thoughts, of one person to the brain of another.

This was one of the forerunners of the grain technology that we see in many previous episodes. The only problem however, was that this first experiment failed. While the memory of one mouse did not transfer to another, the other mouse did feel pain not directly inflicted on it. If the first mouse was pricked with a sharp object, the other would react. Not wanting this vital research to go to waste, Rolo Haynes presents Dr. Dawson with an implant that would allow him to feel the pain of his patients, called the Symphatic Diagnoser.

Dr. Dawson jumps at the chance, and gets the surgery to place the implant in the back of his head. How it works, is that the doctor's implant becomes the receiver of the sensations, and the patients would wear the transmitter—the aforementioned hairnet-like device. Dr. Dawson could then proceed to diagnose patients far more precisely, accessing what they felt, and treating them appropriately. And for a while, everything worked out just fine. TCKR benefited from the vital research and lives were saved. But of course this is *Black Mirror*.

On one occasion, the doctor was hooked up to a patient who went into cardiac arrest, dying in the emergency room. And Dr. Dawson felt every sensation of death, blacking out from the pain. He didn't die, but he felt what it was like to. Now, the thing about death is that when we die, a large amount of neurotransmitters are released all at once. So what Dr. Dawson ended up experience was one giant cocktail of painkillers. Highly addictive painkillers. This starts Dawson on a downward spiral, more concerned with chasing that high, than saving his patients.

At his lowest point, Dawson attacks a homeless man, forcibly putting the receiver device on him, and taking a power drill to the man's skull. The homeless man died, and the doctor slipped into a coma due to the intense sensations. However sad the outcome, this doesn't stop the march of progress. TCKR, despite the ethically questionable pursuits, would continue to develop this technology. But back to the museum.

Next, Rolo tells Nish the story of a young couple, Jack and Carrie. The two had met at a house party and, after a few years, have a child together. Unfortunately one day, while trying to get a better angle for a picture of Jack and their young son, a truck hits Carrie, leaving her in a coma. Jack, devastated, visits her often in St. Junipers hospital, but is only able to communicate with her through a neurological machine with Yes or No responses. It was called a "com-box" and was likely the result of further technological developments of TCKR Systems.

This is where Rolo Haynes comes in, once again. He introduces himself to Jack, and making him an offer. Rolo proposes to transfer the consciousness of Carrie, from her comatose body, to Jack's brain. He explains that since humans do not use more than 40 percent of their brains, it is technically possible to house the consciousness of two people in one body. Of course, this would so Carrie could be able to feel again. She would be able to see her son Parker again. The catch, of course, was that Carrie's physical body would have to be euthanized. Suspicious, Jack was reluctant to give an answer, but the com box signals yes—Carrie's consent at a chance to live again.

With both their consent, the procedure is undertaken and Carrie's consciousness is implanted within Jack's. Much like the cookies from previous episodes, Carrie is visualized as sitting in a chair behind her husband's eyes. There, she was able to feel his sensations, taste food that he ate, and most importantly feel a hug that Parker gave their son, Jack. And everything was fine, at least for a while. Every couple argues from time to time and needs to take a break. But, how do you do that if they are literally in your head?

Carrie and Jack begin to have arguments on, well, pretty much everything. From the most trivial thing like turning the pages too slowly on a comic book, to wandering eyes on the street. Even when you are seeing through the eyes of someone else, it doesn't mean you will see eye to eye on everything. Parker especially was the focal point for a few of their arguments, since Carrie's thought that Jack was dealing with him too harshly over a minor mishap. The instinct of the mother to protect the son was there, even in code.

It got so bad, that Jack went back to Rolo, asking for a solution to this future set of first world problems. The remedy was more control, and of course there was an app for that. Jack could use the TCKR app to mute Carrie, much like you mute a participant on a Zoom call. And he used it. When Carrie got too argumentative, Jack muted her—sometimes for weeks. After an argument over their son, he muted her for months. Months. After a while, they had to come to a compromise. Jack would live his life during the week, with Carrie on mute. Then, during the weekend, he would activate her so she could be with her son. Sort of like a digital joint custody situation. And for a while, that was effective. At least until Jack got a new neighbor.

Emily, who recently moved next door, had caught

Jack's attention. They began talking, and eventually entered into a relationship. Understandably, this would be a problem for Carrie. The actual Carrie was gone, but to her they were still married. Imagine getting a stream of arguments that you can't run away from. Well, that's what Jack's inner life had become. While he was taking care of Parker—and Emily was understanding—Carrie was not letting Jack move on. At his wits end, Jack returned to Rolo's office, asking for yet another solution.

Jack didn't want to delete Carrie from his head. He said that it would be like killing her. Rolo Haynes new solution then, would be to transfer Carrie out of Jack's head, into something else—a stuffed monkey. This monkey, would not be able to communicate fully, rather pared down to only two possible responses. An expression of happiness, or an expression of sadness. This would be to cut down on potential arguments. And they gave the monkey as a gift to Parker, so his mom could still be near him. Realizing that this had been done to her, Carrie goes off, tapping both emotional response buttons to show her outrage.

Emily, witnessing this, takes the toy from Parker, and has a talk in the hallway with Carrie. Being fed up with Carrie being a third wheel in their relationship, she had had more than her fill. Emily threatens Carrie with deletion, unless she agrees to behave. Not wanting to "die" again, Carrie decides to not give the couple any more trouble when it comes to outbursts. Seeing someone threaten a stuffed animal had to be one of the most hilarious scenes in this episode.

What wasn't funny was that Rolo Haynes had actually committed a crime. It had been found out that he had transferred human consciousness into limited form, and that was illegal. He was ousted from the company and forced to find another way to support himself.

And that leads to the final piece of this three-part story. Freelancing, Rolo Haynes gets it in his mind that he will use the technology that he helped pioneer, to open a digital museum of deceased celebrity likenesses. The plan would fall through though, mostly due to management rights and the estates of celebrities keeping Rolo from using them. His solution? Get people who were not so famous, of course.

The final attraction of the Black Museum turns out to be a digital holographic projection of a man named Clayton Leigh. Clayton Leigh was an innocent Black man who had been given the electric chair for the murder of a weather reporter. Clayton, who was on death row, was out of options in many ways. And in comes Haynes, using the man's desperation to his advantage. He promises Clayton a way to secure the financial security of his family—by making a digital clone of his likeness for his museum. Rolo promised that Clayton's family would receive the lion's share of proceeds from the digital image museum he was building. At first, he wants nothing to do with Rolo, and Clayton's wife, Angelica, was highly skeptical as well. But after some convincing, he agrees, not seeing any other way out.

Clayton's appeal is denied, and he's scheduled to be executed. Before the switch is thrown, a device to copy Clayton's consciousness and essence is placed on the side of his temple. In what is akin to making a copy, and shredding the original, Clayton Leigh is executed, while Rolo Haynes secures an exact digital replica of the doomed man.

Instead of just keeping Clayton's digital image as an attraction however, Rolo re-frames it to allow visitors of the museum to throw the electric chair switch on him. Over and over again. What the visitors see, is guilty man on death row, and they have the opportunity to punish him themselves. The machine has a 10 second limit, as it's explained that any longer and the digital Clayton's mind would break—no good for future use. As a macabre bonus, the machine that executes Clayton's digital image produces a souvenir of his suffering on a key chain, forever freezing him in the moment of death. This is similar to the lynching post cards of the early 20th Century, except worse. Eventually, one of the visitors throws the switch for 14 seconds, in effect turning Clayton's hologram into a vegetable. In the future, not too different from now, there are still people who get a disgusting thrill out of seeing Black people suffer.

But soon, it would be Rolo's turn to suffer. Unbeknownst to him, Nish is a tech savvy individual, and she was no random visitor at all. Before entering the museum, Nish had planted a miniature device that knocks out the entire air conditioning system for the museum. While Rolo is telling Nish all of these stories, she offers him a bottle of water. What he didn't know, is that the bottle of water was poisoned, and that it would take some time to work through his system.

And in the time that it had taken for Rolo Haynes to get visibly sick, he had in essence confessed to all of these crimes. Too weak to fight back, Nish sits Rolo down in a chair, right in front of the burned out holographic image of Clayton, to explain what was happening and why. It's then, that the masks slips. Nish is Clayton's daughter.

While in the chair, Nish explains to Rolo all the things that he left out of his story. He left out the protests that turned his viable business into one that was struggling, on the wane. She also mentioned that Rolo had allowed many unsavory people to throw the switch on Clayton well over the 10-second limit, which is what resulted in him being in the vegetative, drooling state. Also left out, was the fate of his wife Angelica, who came to visit Clayton and couldn't handle seeing him like that. She wound up overdosing on pills, taking her own life.

While the poison in Rolo's system works to end his life, Nish pulls a miniature computer out of her knapsack. Putting the grain device on the side of his temple, she copies his consciousness and puts it with her father. And after confirming that his consciousness is awake, she pulls the switch, killing both the digital hologram of her dad and Rolo Haynes. She refers to it as a "double-decker mercy killing."

Afterwards, she rescues the stuffed monkey from the museum, unplugs the device from the digital AC, and watches as an electrical fire burned down the museum. And before she pulls off, we see her having a conversation with her mother, who was in her head the whole time. Nish, even though her mom committed suicide, was able to save her digital consciousness.

"Black Museum" is one of the most powerful episodes of *Black Mirror*, tackling many themes including justice, retribution, and the enduring nature of American racism. Science fiction can be Utopian, but not often. The world still has people without health insurance, homeless, and a criminal justice system overly punitive to Black people. It cuts against the technocratic notion that better technology will, in of itself, produce a fairer world.

If you really take it apart and analyze it, Black Museum and White Bear are at opposite ends of the punitive spectrum. White Bear is about an ongoing punishment of the complicit and guilty, while Black Museum is about the death and posthumous digital suffering of the innocent.

We see how Rolo Haynes preys on the desperate and the vulnerable, and that he has done so his whole career. In this museum of futuristic crime, he is the architect. This episode, in a way, was Rolo exposing his own culpability and getting what he deserved. Exploitative, bigoted, crass, and misogynistic Rolo Haynes is a recognizable archetype. And unfortunately, people like him will continue to exist, since the underpinnings of bigotry and prejudice don't necessarily vanish as the years and decades go by.

In thinking about the episode, it brings forth the notion of social death. It's a concept that comes from slavery, and depicts how the lives of the enslaved are not their own. In the book *Slavery and Social Death* by Orlando Patterson, Patterson points out the number of ways in which the enslaved were not regarded as full human beings. If living, breathing Black people aren't thought of as human, than a digital copy of one of us would be considered as even less.

Now extrapolate this into the near future. First of all, it is a society where the death penalty still exists, and secondly, the rights of the disadvantaged are violated even in death. Knowing the nature of

American racism, it's not too far off that some would want a souvenir commemorating Black suffering and death.

Historical memory is also a powerful theme here. Rolo Haynes believes that he's meeting someone with no cultural or historical memory, and can just rattle off about how "justice was served" in the execution of Clayton Leigh. The memories of the people who were wronged were left out of his retelling. The shattered families, the campaigns against his museum, all of it left on the cutting room floor. Much like the point made in the 2005 Apartheid documentary *We Remember Differently*, Nish and Rolo recall the past through differing social lenses.

Historical memory and personal memory often intersect. We can see this when Nish is driving, listening to the Dionne Warwick version of the song "Always Something There To Remind Me." We didn't know it in the beginning, but she could have been listening to the song as a request from her mom.

While it is a powerful story of a daughter avenging her wrongfully executed father, there's something else that went on here. Rolo Haynes was cut loose from TCKR, and the company itself continued on with no consequences. This really shows the reality of how, even when individual racists are exposed and punished, the institutions are allowed to continue on.

Netflix Special: Bandersnatch

Aired: December 28, 2018
Director: David Slade
Writer: Charlie Brooker
Producer: Russell McLean
Cast: Fionn Whitehead (Stefan Butler), Craig Parkinson (Peter Butler), Will Pouter (Colin Ritman), Alice Lowe (Dr. Haynes), Asim Chaudhry (Mohan Thakur)

"I know I can do it proper justice." – Stefan Butler

Have you ever felt like, no matter what choices you make, some occurrences in your life are just pre-determined? Game programmer Stefan Butler confronts this feeling in *Black Mirror: Bandersnatch. Bandersnatch* is different from every other *Black Mirror* episode, in that it is an interactive movie. At key moments in the plot, the viewer must make decisions for Stefan. The choices made, large or small, lead to different endings.

Set in 1984, *Bandersnatch* tells us the story of a young man who was given the rare opportunity to make a game based on one of his favorite books. A computer programmer, Stefan is enthralled with the novel, *Bandersnatch*. Written by Jerome F. Davies, it's a choose your own adventure story where the protagonist needs to make their way through a maze, while also having to avoid a blue demon. The book has different endings, depending on what you do, and so Stefan is creating a role-playing game with a similar concept. Although, how the episode plays out depends on you, the viewer—a choose your own adventure.

Early morning on July 9th, Stefan starts his day preparing for a meeting with the emerging gaming company Tuckersoft. At breakfast with his dad, he's barely paying attention, thumbing through the book instead of eating. We're introduced to the concept of choice, being asked to decide what he'll have for breakfast, as well as which tape he plays on his Walkman. Stefan eventually meets with the head of Tuckersoft, Mohan Thakur, to show off a demo of his game.

Mohan introduces Stefan to Colin Ritman, the leading game designer of Tuckersoft. An accomplished programmer and famous, Stefan looks up to him in a sense. When they first meet, Colin is working on a game called "Nohzdyve," an obvious reference to the first episode of Season 3. After a bit of chit chat about game design theories and philosophers, the viewer is confronted with the first large choice of the film—Mohan offers to grant space for Stefan to write the game in their brand new, imposing office. He explains that Stefan would be given a full team, and would have access to all of the resources of Tuckersoft.

As repeat viewers—or players—of "Bandersnatch" will find out, Stefan writing the video game himself is the choice that the film wants you to choose. If you choose to do the game with Tuckersoft, the game won't do well, due to the rushed nature of it. A little commentary on how producers can ruin creative vision. Colin will even tell you that you took the wrong path.

While interactive, it becomes clear that the viewer is being steered in particular directions. Once Stefan declines the offer to do the game at Tuckersoft headquarters, he gets the backing of Colin Ritman, who understands the need for his creative process to be respected. He even recommends a set of albums for Stefan to listen to, to help with his programming work.

Now Stefan is under pressure, but not just because of his big game creation opportunity. As he works on his game, it's coming up on the anniversary of his mother's death. The story here is that Stefan's mom was supposed to catch a train at 8:15 a.m., but was late because he was looking for his stuffed rabbit. Because of the delay, his mom had to take the 8:45 a.m. train, which got into an accident. This has become a source of anxiety for Stefan, and he blames his father for hiding the rabbit from him.

Finding himself stuck in a creative slump, Stefan meets up with Colin. To get himself out of "The Hole" as he calls it, Colin recommends mind-altering drugs. Users who choose to have Stefan take the tablet are treated to a weird psychedelic trip, during which Colin breaks down an elaborate theory of how there are different realities. He gets into this notion of a cosmic flow chart that determines where you can and can't go, ranting about how we really don't have free will as human beings. He likens it to Pac-man, which he says stands for "Program and Control."

I'll give Colin this: it was an interesting theory of the world and reality that he presented. Well, more so force fed then presented, but the point still holds. How

Colin's rant about differing realities relates to the game that Stefan is working on is a non sequitur, but it is an interesting aside. But it's also analogous to how we're watching the film, making choices for something that's already been pre-determined.

This is fairly common when it comes to what people want to embrace. Colin symbolizes a moment of awakening for Stefan. He had been walking around, accepting things as they are, which has robbed him of his creative muse. Colin was the Morpheus to Stefan's Neo, showing him the truth of the world. The key difference though is at least Neo had a choice. Bringing someone to your home and spiking their tea with LSD tablets is all types of wrong. The conversations around consent that we have nowadays just weren't had in 1984.

Stefan does not get a chance to come down from the acid trip however, and Colin offers one final decision for us to make—since nothing matters, Colin walks towards the terrace of his apartment and asks Stefan who is jumping off the roof. Wanting to see what would happen, I first chose to have Colin jump.

What is most noticeable is the nihilistic nature of this episode. You're encouraged to mess up Stefan's life and yet there is virtually no way to avoid doing so. In fact, the worst choices seem to yield the most desirable outcomes. If you don't tell Stefan to take his meds, kill his dad, and chop the body up, you get a better game than you do if you play it safe. Maybe we like to vicariously ruin lives? Is this what the interactive movie is exploring? Could be.

I found myself—just out of sheer curiosity—looking into if there was actually a book called Bandersnatch. There is, but not in the way depicted in the film. The notion of the creature known as the Bandersnatch emerges originally from the Lewis Carroll children's novel *Through The Looking Glass*. It is a sequel to *Alice in Wonderland*, where Alice ventures to another realm of existence by climbing through a mirror. The creature is depicted as a fire-breathing monster. The only book with the title *Bandersnatch* is a collaborative effort between C.S. Lewis, and J.R.R. Tolkien. And just like there are YouTube rabbit holes one can fall down, this is one of them. So I tried looking into the definition of the word, of which there are two:

1. an imaginary wild animal of fierce disposition.
2. a person of uncouth or unconventional habits, attitudes, etc., especially one considered a menace, nuisance, or the like.

Well, the first definition fits pretty well with the episode, since we see so many appearances of this blue demon. Whether it's a random jump scare, or an image, it plays a part. The second definition is also worth noting, as it gives one pause to think, what is considered unconventional and uncouth in this society? Is it a person who cannot be controlled? Is it the individual who chooses not from the choices presented to them?

After playing through it a few times, I believe that there is a true message of *Bandersnatch*. I deliberately choose the word play here, because it's more like a game than a film. You take a path, see what happens. You go back, make another choice, and see if anything turns out differently. It's a different experience each time, and if we go along with Colin's musing that there are messages in every game, then there are certainly messages in this interactive film/game as well.

A game—unlike real life—has rules that the players have to abide by. In real life, not so much. Everything is so arbitrary and there are too many gray areas. Sometimes, during my gaming sessions with Grand Theft Auto, I have thought to myself that I have more options in this game than in real life. For those of us who can't do helicopter rides, a virtual one will do. No one should feel like we have more options in a game than in real life, but that's how it is. I'm not saying that people should shoot rocket-propelled grenades at random vehicles for real, but it's fun to do it in a game. Just saying. Anyway, back to my larger point.

The choice trees—represented by the block like icon with two prongs—represents the division of our lives into the binary. Much like Stefan, our essential choices are constrained to just two, no more. We must choose, we're told. If we get indignant about the choices we are presented with, we're told to hush, and to stop being petulant.

Life is presented as either a one or zero. On or off. Democrat or Republican. Working poverty or complete destitution. Compliance or punishment. There are no alternatives, is what we are constantly told. Anything else falls outside of the parameters of thinkable thought. To choose another choice, outside of the ones presented to you, evokes the rage of everyone else. If you decide not to choose at all, heaven help you. Off to the digital cornfield you go—canceled, banished, and ostracized for all to see.

Even when the choices get worse, you are supposed to choose. Even when the choices you are presented with are inadequate, and don't speak to your needs, you have to choose. And should you choose wrong? You're told that you will somehow doom everyone else in the process. We are encouraged to choose the best of bad choices, and that is the marker of being realistic in these modern times.

You have a great deal of trivial choices in "Bandersnatch," but nothing you do will take the protagonist off of his destructive path. A different choice is just not in the cards—or the script. In our modern lives, you can choose from eight or nine different types of toothpaste, but the more important choices are constrained to very few. It's like being forced to keep playing a rigged game, where you know that it's rigged. And if you don't play, you're punished. Doesn't sound like much fun, when you really get right down to it.

What's interesting about this episode though, is that it's about a designer making a video game based on a book. As you go along, you realize the comedy in seeing the process of a fictional game being created for a fictional company, with the game being based on a fictional book that was never written, by an author that doesn't exist. It's a tragedy that we all took some small part in the film, and unwillingly take part in real life. It's symbolic of the way in which all of us are similarly boxed in, as we watch conditions worsen around us.

Bandersnatch is about having your real options constrained, while at the same time being presented with a bevy of meaningless choices. The sad reality is that, in some cases, there are more choices in past times then there are for life paths. So why not play around with someone's life in an interactive virtual manner? At least you can start a fight and make it interesting.

Season 5

Episode 1: Striking Vipers

Aired: June 5th, 2019
Director: Owen Harris
Writer: Charlie Brooker
Cast: Anthony Mackie (Danny Parker), Yahya Abdul-Mateen II (Karl Houghton), Nicole Beharie (Theo Parker), Pom Klementieff (Roxette), Ludin Lin (Lance)

"You have to brace yourself." – Karl Houghton

Round 1… Fight! The world of video games draws millions of people into their alternate realities every year. And "Striking Vipers," Danny Parker and Karl Houghton would find out more about each other than they expected.

This episode begins at a club where Danny is talking to Theo at the bar. The two are role playing, pretending not to know one another to make things more interesting. Once Karl shows up with his date, they drop the façade and head to the dance floor together. Their night ends with them sleeping together, all revved up from earlier.

When Danny wakes up the next morning, he catches Karl smoking weed and playing a game called

Striking Vipers. Karl challenges him to a game and it's as simple as that. Challenge accepted. After a few rounds go by, they get loud, and start roughhousing with one another. They end up being so loud that they wind up waking Theo. Danny stops the game, and tries to apologize. But not before Karl teases him for getting scolded and play humps him as a joke. There's always a tell here and there.

The story flashes forward to their post-college life, where they've reunited after 11 years. Danny, who is more traditional minded, is now married to Theo and has settled down with a child in the suburbs. Karl on the other hand, is still out there playing the field, dating women younger than him. For his 38th birthday, Karl brings him a gift—Striking Vipers X and the virtual reality headpiece that goes along with it. On the box, the letters TCKR appear. While they catch up a bit, we learn that Danny has developed a bad knee, preventing him from being as physically active as he would like.

The episode focuses on showing two divergent lives of old friends. In the years that have passed, Danny's built a life for himself, that in some ways he feels trapped by. And Karl is always looking for that thrill, and is much less concerned about commitment. Escapist pursuits often find their way into people's lives to fulfill that sense of longing for something else, and we see how literal that becomes the first time that Danny and Karl load up Striking Vipers X.

When they sit down for the first time, Karl warns Danny to brace himself. He's tested the game out in the store, and knows what they're in for. Danny puts the card inside of the controller and the virtual reality disc

The Binge Watcher's Guide to Black Mirror

on the side of his head. The game boots up and it's time to choose their characters. Karl picks Roxette, a Chun Li-type character to compliment Danny's pick of Lance, clearly inspired by Ryu from Street Fighter. And once he presses the sync button, Danny's eyes go grey.

Danny is transported into the game world, landing in a fully immersive dojo. This sequence is a mental trip, as Danny notices that his knee is giving him no discomfort while in the game. As they begin the match, Karl flexes his experience with the game and straight beats on Danny. Imagine getting punched in a fighting game and feeling the sensation in real life. No real life harm is done, but the game reflects Danny's character with facial bruises and a bloody lip. It doesn't take much for Karl to win their first round.

The damage resets for the second round, and while Danny tries to put up more of a fight, it doesn't work out. He's beyond rusty. But, he does get in a few more hits here and there. Eventually, as he gets more into the groove of the game, he finally starts blocking some of Karl's moves. Both characters end up on the ground, rolling around exhausted. And when Karl's character Roxette winds up on top of Danny's, they kiss.

For a moment, Danny enjoys it, but quickly remembers himself and pushes Karl away. Totally freaked out, by both the situation and himself, he asks his friend how to get out of the game. Roxette says "Exit Game!" and is transported out. Seconds later, Danny does the same and comes to, feeling a certain way about what happened.

A night later, they load up the game again. Danny gets on the headset and tells Karl that he was drunk last night. So they hop into the game, both pretending that they're going to just fight, but by the second round not a punch is thrown—they just start going at it. Their characters have sex with one another in the game for the first time, and they get the full experience, even talking in the afterglow moment. Their conversation is interrupted by Danny's son kicking him in the leg, booting him from the game. He was up, and wanted some water.

This romp goes on for a bit, but the signs of something going on start showing. Danny is a lot more distracted and finds himself often staring into nothing, thinking of these encounters. We see him distracted at work, pulling back from socializing with co-workers, and worse he stops having sex with Theo. His new "relationship" is siphoning energy from his real life commitments, distancing him from his wife.

After weeks of this, Theo begins to wonder if it's her. We see her in the mirror, looking at herself and the shape of her body. Intuitively, she senses that something is up with the physically and emotionally distant behavior of her husband. And so she confronts him at their wedding anniversary dinner.

Theo asks Danny if anything is going on, to which he denies and promises that he's not seeing anyone else. In a very interesting departure from many couple's arguments, Theo starts talking about the sacrifices that couples have to make for things to work. How closing the door on life "out there" is necessary to build up a life with someone. Essentially, it's a reminder of the principle of "forsaking all others" when you are married—a vow that Danny was violating, even if only virtually.

It's at this point that Danny decides to break off his virtual entanglement once and for all. He calls Karl

The Binge Watcher's Guide to Black Mirror

and tells him that he can't do it anymore. Karl doesn't want to end it, but Danny is done. He puts the virtual reality disc up on the shelf and doesn't play the game at all for seven months. As far as he is concerned, this is all behind him.

And it was—at least until Danny's next birthday celebration. Theo, who didn't know about what was going on, invites Karl to their home for dinner. The look on Danny's face when Theo tells him is a non-verbal iteration of "Wait, what?" Too late to cancel, and not wanting to make Theo suspect anything, Danny pushes forward with the get together. The next scene makes this episode hilarious, as Danny and Karl fake smile at each other until Theo goes into the kitchen to get dessert. They get into one of those whispering arguments, with Karl voicing that he misses it all. He says that he tried to do it virtually with other players, but it just wasn't the same. All "competition" is not created equal, we suppose. Karl's desperation hit a low point with his next confession.

"You know, I even fucked Tundra the polar bear character. I fucked a polar bear and still couldn't get you out of my mind." Bruh! None of us were ready for that. Danny doesn't even look at Karl, staring straight in front of him at the table and responds that he can't help him. But Karl still persists.

He offers Danny another game of solo "Heroes vs. Villains," telling him to meet him online at midnight. He even gets in his ear to try to entice him, only to have Danny grab his shoulder and push him back into his seat. Just seconds later, Theo walks back in with a puzzled look. If she only knew.

Danny ends up taking Karl's offer. Getting out of

bed, he loads the game up for the midnight match where, of course, they go at it again. At least until Karl—as Roxette—messes up and says "I love you." Danny pushes away, not knowing how to deal with that one. As spelled out by the big "Game Over" sign behind them, this can't last.

Danny decides to meet with Karl in real life, to see what it is. What he wants is to kiss, for real, and find out if the connection they have for one another is more than just a game. After much hesitation, they do, but there's no spark. Danny wants to break it off completely at this point, yet Karl does not. They end up getting into a fist fight over it, getting themselves arrested. And when Theo comes to bail him out, he has to explain why they were fighting in the first place. That ride back must have been awkward.

The episode ends with a compromise: Karl and Danny can have their online romp, in exchange for Theo being able to deal with a guy on the side as well. On Danny's birthday, Theo gives him the game, just before she gets to take her wedding ring off for just that night. Not wanting to break up, with two children, they come to an understanding—compromise is all a part of the game, I suppose.

While it's a decent episode, it doesn't pack as much of a punch as "San Junipero." I kept thinking to myself "Hey, that's Falcon from *The Aven*gers and Abbie Mills from *Sleepy Hollow*!" It was this episode that I started to realize that some of the big names that *Black Mirror* was starting to cast was taking me out of the story.

This episode makes you think about what infidelity means, and if it goes beyond the physical.

You get it, when you really sit back and think about it. Once you get past the initial shock, the appeal is understandable. The idea of getting all the sensations of sex, without the possibility of contracting a sexually transmitted disease, is enough for people to want this to become a real thing. Those GG or "good game" post-match messages will hit a little differently if this ever comes to pass, that's for sure.

Fun Fact: Speaking of games, the name "Striking Vipers" is reminiscent of this old game on Sega Saturn called Fighting Vipers. The game engine was based on the Virtual Fighter series, but this game never really took off.

Episode 2: Smithereens

Aired: June 5th, 2019
Director: James Hawes
Writer: Charlie Brooker
Cast: Andrew Scott (Christopher Gillhaney), Damson Idris (Jaden Tommins), Topher Grace (Billy Bauer), Monica Dolan (CS Linda Grace), Amanda Drew (Haley Blackwood), Daniel Ings (David Gilkes), Ruibo Qian (Penelope Wu)

"The sky could turn fucking purple and you cunts wouldn't notice for a month." –Christopher Gillhaney

In this episode, we have yet another cautionary tale. "Smithereens" follows a middle-aged man who has used his gig as a driver to take a hostage. Christopher Gillhaney is a disturbed man wanting to use this leverage to speak with the founder of Smithereens, Billy Bauer. Set in 2018 in London, "Smithereens" is quite possible today, much like "Shut Up and Dance."

As the episode begins, we see Christopher as a person who is just trying to do his job, but wracked with personal anxiety. He listens to guided meditation, trying to ease his mind as he goes about his gig. A gig that we quickly learn he is using with purpose. Christopher picks up a woman coming out of the Smithereens building. During the ride, he asks if she works for the company, but she explains that she does not. Christopher, disappointed, has wasted his time.

We next see Christopher eating in a diner, with people and their phones buzzing all around him. The whole experience is perking his anxiety, and he looks on the verge of having a panic attack. Obviously, there is something that he isn't dealing with.

Appropriately, we next see Christopher in a grief counseling session. He doesn't speak, but we learn that he is there because he lost someone close to him. Who does speak is Hayley, a mother who lost her daughter to suicide 18 months ago. There had been no previous indication of anything being wrong, and Hayley is dealing with the agony of not knowing why. It's a mix of anger and grief, because she just wishes that her daughter would have come to her with it.

After the counseling session, the two talk privately. She asks about his story, but he hasn't found the right moment. Hayley invites him back to her place for coffee, to which he at first hesitates, claiming he has to work tomorrow. But after making an awkward joke, he obliges her, and they end up sleeping with one another.

The following morning, Hayley tells him more about her daughter. He discovers that she has been trying to gain access to her Persona account—a Facebook like social media—to get clues. Understandably, she's fixated on finding out in hopes that the account might possibly give a reason as to why she might have killed herself. She has a notebook of password guesses, and tries to guess three times a day, before the system locks her out.

The next customer Christopher has is just the

The Binge Watcher's Guide to Black Mirror

kind of person he was searching for. Jaden, who works for Smithereens as an intern, gets into the car. Notably, the building is on Skillane Street, yet another Easter egg item for fans to pick up on. After Jaden confirms that he works for the company, Christopher then initiates his plan. Citing that the system has alerted him to an accident up ahead, he asks Jaden if it's alright that he take an alternative path to avoid the pile up. Jaden, not looking up from his phone agrees, and Christopher switches the destination.

By the time Jaden looks up and realize where he is, Christopher has pulled his gun on him, and tells him to put on plastic handcuffs.

After learning that Jaden is only an intern, Christopher goes off on a rant about modern companies and hierarchy. He had thought Jaden was a high level employee because of his suit, but this was just his first week and Jaden had wanted to make an impression. It must be scary witnessing a man rant at you with a gun in his hand. When Christopher turns his back, Jaden tries to escape, but fails.

Christopher catches up with him, threatening to kill him right then and there, and forces him to get into the trunk of a second car. After a few seconds in the trunk though, Jaden panics, saying that he can't be in small places. Surprisingly, Christopher lets him out, telling him to get in the back seat instead, and to lay down with a cloth bag over his head. Christopher may be deranged and desperate, but he's not a hardened criminal.

Unfortunately for Christopher—but fortunately for Jaden—a police officer spots Jaden with a bag over his head as they drive by. Seeing that the police are following him now, Christopher pulls over and acts like he is going to let the police stop him. The two police officers see that he is not getting out of the car, and figure that he was going to run. While they sit there, waiting for him to do something, one of the officers take his license plate numbers. And as soon as one of them step out of their squad car, Christopher pulls off. So the police chase begins.

They pursue Christopher and only stop when he has to swerve to avoid two teenagers on bikes. Now stranded out in a field, the police approach his car—without a gun—telling him to step out of the car. He complies, pointing his gun towards Jaden and telling the police to back off or the kid dies. This is now a full-fledged hostage situation. That fact is radioed in, and the police call for back up.

Pressing forward with the reason for the kidnapping, Christopher has Jaden contact his people in Smithereens to get in contact with the owner, Billy Bauer. Jaden left his phone in the other car, meaning Christopher has to use his own. When they finally reach a live person, Christopher grabs it and demands to speak to the head of the company. To confirm that it wasn't a prank, he sends a picture of Jaden in the backseat of his car, with the gun pointed at him. At that point, realizing that this is a credible threat, more authorities get involved.

The police call in a negotiator, and more officers with sniper rifles. Their first inclination is to try and talk to Christopher, to see what he wants, but they have their backup plan in place. While all this is happening, he is still on hold with Smithereens. The company by now has ran a cross reference on his social media profile, pulling everything that could be useful to the police. And while they have him on hold, they are listening to everything happening in the car. They even have a voice to text transcript of what's being said. After stalling as long as they could, the company puts him on the line with Penelope Wu, their chief operating officer. Penelope, following protocol, protects the head of the company. She attempts to find out what the call was about, but Christopher is deadly serious about only speaking with Billy Bauer. He threatens to kill Jaden again and tells them to stop playing around.

On the other end of things, the police find out his name and key details of his recent life. They discover that Christopher is staying at his late mother's house and that he was a former teacher. They mention him being involved in a car accident, the victim of a drunk driver. They share these details with the negotiator, who is hoping to talk Christopher out of doing anything crazy. But before they get a chance to, they get a call from the FBI. Now they're involved, as Smithereens is a Silicon Valley based company.

Everyone is sharing information to learn as much about Christopher as they can. It just goes to show how easily people's information can be found when the spotlight appears on their personal life nowadays. As they dig deeper into his social media record, they find that he lost his fiancée in the previously mentioned car crash. From that, they assemble a whole psychological profile on the fly. The targeting of the Smithereens employees was deliberate, but Christopher registered the Hitcher account under another name. Armed with that information, the lead negotiator approaches the car slowly.

Using a bullhorn to talk to Christopher, the negotiator tries to reason with him. He follows up with a phone call which backfires, pissing Christopher off. He knows what negotiators do, and he's not falling for it. He once again threatens to kill Jaden if the negotiator doesn't get into his car and drive away. The police, not wanting to take the chance, order him to leave. Jaden is still in danger, and the police snipers don't have a clear shot.

Meanwhile, the company seems to have little choice other than to reach Billy Bauer. This next bit of detail is what makes this episode the most ironic. See, Billy is the head of the company, but is on a no contact, detox for 10 days. Of all the times to be on vacation. It's like he took part in creating this monster, but has the luxury of getting away from it all—unlike a lot of us. Only because the life of one of their employees is on the line, does it even get to him directly.

By this time, the incident is all over social media now, as well as the mainstream news. To comfort Jaden, Christopher tells him that the gun is not real. The police overhear that however, and start to make a move. Now, it looks like they are about to move in and rescue Jaden. Until he lets off a warning shot in the air, to let the cops know the gun is real.

When Christopher does finally get the chance to speak to Billy, he tells him the story of how he lost his fiancée. Apparently, it was his fault. He was a heavy user of the Smithereens app. On a long drive back from visiting his mom, he got a notification, and in the short time he glanced at his phone to see what it was, the drunk driver crashed into him. He felt culpable for this, not wanting to divulge it to anyone. Not the grief counseling group he was part of, and definitely not her mom. Two years later, he was still reeling from the reality that his boredom played a role in the demise of his fiancée.

It's a very plausible and terrible thing to reckon with. So terrible, that Christopher is planning to let Jaden go, and off himself. Billy tries to talk him out of it, but before he does, he gets a favor. He gets access to the Persona account of Hayley's daughter. A kind gesture of closure, to another grieving person.

Jaden struggles with Christopher for the gun to try and stop him from killing himself at the same time that the police take their shot. But we don't know who gets hit. We suppose someone's life has ended and become just another notification on everyone's phones. This episode is reminiscent of "Falling Down," with a man spiraling out of control and left to his own devices. He individually goes in a bad direction, and his life may have been ended. Or the hostage he took. We don't really know.

This episode raises concerns about the effects of social media that were recently highlighted in the documentary "The Social Dilemma." The question: are you using social media, or is social media using you?

Episode 3: Rachel, Jack, and Ashley Too

Aired: June 5th, 2019
Director: Anne Sewitsky
Writer: Charlie Brooker
Cast: Miley Cyrus (Ashley O), Angourie Rice (Rachel), Madison Davenport (Jack), Susan Pourfar (Catherine), Marc Menchaca (Kevin), Jerah Milligan (Busy G)

"She doesn't understand how fragile this all is"
- Catherine

"Rachel, Jack, and Ashley Too" is the story of three young women, all at different stages of their lives, as they struggle to just be themselves. Rachel, a teenage girl who feels like an outsider is the new girl at school, and lacks confidence, often sits by herself in the cafeteria. Her elder sister Jack is set in who she is and is far more jaded. Both are coping with the reality of life after losing their mom. As for Ashley—played by Miley Cyrus—hers is a life of caged luxury and stardom.

Feeling like a loner and hating being the new kid in school, Rachel finds comfort in Ashley O's music, most of which is carefully managed, positive affirming messages. Pop culture has always been geared towards the youth, and Rachel is in that prime targeted demographic. Completely enamored with Ashley O, she sings her songs and even starts to dress like her. It really goes to show how pop stars are as much brand as artists.

Ashley O's personality is upbeat, bubbly, and takes a can-do attitude towards anything in life. As typified in the hit song "I'm on a Roll," Ashley O's confidence is an anthem—one tailor made to ring true with many. But that's the thing, it's all tailor made. From her lyrics down to what she wears and how she acts.

On a talk show appearance, Ashley O debuts a new product, a robot doll based on her personality— Ashley Too. It's a doll that can have conversations with their owner, and learn their likes and dislikes based on those conversation. It's a digital companion where you have a piece of your favorite pop star all to yourself. Of course, being the super fan that she is, Rachel asks her dad for the doll for her 15th birthday. In an un-boxing reminiscent of what we often see on YouTube, Rachel sets up the doll. It asks her questions, learns her personality and gives her ways to boost her self-esteem.

There's even a smartphone app that teaches Rachel how to do Ashley O's dance steps. All of this seems well, and harmless enough. But underneath the well-oiled machine that is Ashley O's career, there's the angst that they're dealing with.

Ashley O is managed and mentored by her Aunt Catherine. Her aunt—who became her caretaker after her parents died—is the force behind the brand. A brand that Ashley O is feeling weary of at this point. She wants to change her material, feels trapped as a pop artist. She's stressed, taking meds to deal with her conflicted emotions, and just wants to breathe again.

However, she is obligated via contract to keep going. The pressure is on to continue producing, to keep the façade and fame up. It's a machine and it must be fed.

After an argument about the direction of her music, Ashley finds herself captive by her manager's bottom line. And her bottom-line focused, ruthless aunt has had enough of Ashley O's chafing. At lunch, Ashley is slipped something that puts her into a medically induced coma. And while she's in the coma, Catherine orchestrates the creation of another entire album from her by reading her brain waves.

Using those brain waves, combined with vocal mimicry software, she creates all new music without having to hear any of Ashley's lip. Using footage from past Ashley O concerts, the team even comes up with body scans to create a hologram of her. It's very reminiscent of the Tupac Shakur hologram that was at Coachella back in 2012. Using technology to collate a new album of 10 songs really calls up how record labels have already done similar things with unreleased tracks as posthumous material. The label still has to make their numbers, right?

When Rachel's Ashley Too doll sees a news report that Ashley O is in a coma, the doll malfunctions. Somehow, the dolls limiter becomes turned off, allowing her true personality to come through. Much like the real Ashley, her dolls had been limited in how they could behave—a control mechanism reminiscent of the fourth prime directive in *Robocop* that prevented him from arresting any senior officers in OCP.

Now having full agency, Ashley Too wrangles the two sisters to embark on a mission to rescue the real Ashley O. But this unlikely rescue would yield a plot twist—the doll had tricked the two into helping her, with the intention to pull the plug on the comatose Ashley. The machine she was hooked up to was in actuality maintaining the coma. She claims that she can't bear to see her real self being used by her aunt.

The twins manage to disconnect the real Ashley from the machine and even smuggle her out of the home she was locked up in. A real princess in the tower situation. Meanwhile, Catherine is attempting to put on a show using the hologram to make the actual Ashley obsolete. With her niece out of the way, she would be free to continue pushing the brand the way she wanted to, forever. That is, until the real Ashley crashes her own concert.

Catherine attempts to put Ashley O back under, but fails and ends up being exposed. It feels like a Scooby Doo episode, where teenagers have to foil the evil doing of adults. And just like a cartoon, the episode ends with the three girls rocking out to Ashley's new, rocker look.

Although you can argue that they wanted to frame the episode the way Disney did Miley Cyrus's own show, to draw the parallel between her and her character Ashley O, it feels not quite right for a *Black Mirror* episode. It's also probably the least convincing in terms of plausibility, and definitely the most over-reliant on star power.

While the episode did have its points to make about commercialization and the vapid, transient nature of pop stardom and celebrities, it really fell short in dialogue. There were a few misses here, especially in terms of character development, most of which is given all at once, rather than organically. It's a shame to end on an episode like this, but here we are.

If You Only Watch One Episode

If you were to only watch one episode of *Black Mirror*, I would highly recommend that you give "Nosedive "a chance. It gives so much, in so short a time, and is increasingly closer to reality every day. It's a case study of how social media has become a system that people game, using it to be liked, sell themselves, and promote who they want us to believe they are. "Nosedive" is a cautionary tale on allowing your entire life to be led by how others view you.

Our protagonist, Lacie Pound, is the prototypical people pleaser and social climber that we all know in some shape, and "Nosedive" really hammers home the dangers of living like that. In just one episode, we see Lacie's entire social arc and fall from favor, ending with her practically having a nervous breakdown.

The thing is, being popular or widely liked is a quality that is always fraying at the edges. You chase clout, and relevance, and it works even harder to get away from you. The more you try to be liked, the less authentic you really are. And the pretending never ends, not even for a minute until you decide to get off of the merry go round all together.

The bright, colorful scenery of this episode hides a brutal, technologically refined classism that is always just beneath the surface. This world, like its people, wears a facade of perfection. What might have started as a fun way to connect with others, has turned into a digital prison where thoughts and reactions are monitored. It's a velvet glove covering an iron fist.

On social media, there are aspects of ourselves that we do not reveal publicly. Some of us have the sense that there would be consequences, and "Nosedive" really goes far to show how quickly you can fall out of favor, becoming persona non grata for one bad happenstance. Think of our hyper connected and highly visible social media driven culture. Many of us are one tweet away from people looking at us sideways or questioning everything we've ever said. That silly meme you shared on Instagram five years ago might just become the subject of interest should your profile rise.

With this episode, you can go in not knowing anything about the show and still appreciate everything that it's doing. No, we are not yet at the point where we can be down rated for bumping into someone or making them spill their frappucino. But we do see it in small ways, like when people are eviscerated online for saying something a small set of people disagree with. It can be anything from an off color tweet or an insensitive post about a current event—if someone didn't like it, you're going to hear about it.

In this digital landscape of social media, people have been scorched by their own hot takes. It's really not even that hard for it to happen you—some folks with time on their hands can comb through whatever you might have said until they find objectionable to latch onto. And all of it for the purposes of putting you on blast, characterizing who you are. We see the pettiness of people enabled, and no one is afforded a chance to live things down or grow.

"Nosedive" depicts a society that could be the likely outgrowth of this soft approach to keeping people in line. When a society ties your social potential to your reputation, it becomes less about Big Brother, and more about your neighbors and peers. Imagine being down rated by a person for absolutely no reason, other than they don't like your face. The social credit system can take that into account and then decide what type of apartment and job you get. It's a social credit score, where every stranger is a lender.

What Nosedive also gives us is a reinforcement of class oppression, using technology as an aid. People of higher scores tended to be mostly white and affluent, while the service workers tended to be people of color. Relegated to service jobs, these people tended to be lower rated, such as the nervous Chester who—in a desperate attempt to keep his job—was going out of his way to be overly nice to everyone. And yet he would still find himself on the outs, unable to even enter the building where he worked. The thing is, if anyone can rate anyone, what's to stop people with prejudices from pushing anyone they don't like further down the ladder? And who would stop them? Much like when people are afraid to stand up for someone else in fear of social retribution, this informal system of bullying is backed by institutions.

"Nosedive" also explores the slippery and transitory nature of online friendships. In their interactions—and subsequent disengagement—it becomes clear that Lacey and Naomie knew each other, but weren't really ever friends. They were both using each other to climb that ladder. There was a study done a few years ago that showed that a lot of people we think of as friends, don't necessarily feel the same. Lacey finds this out the hard way, and it's surprisingly devastating on her.

Lacey plays the game and loses, and we empathize with her fall from grace. Was she wrong to play the game? Most of us would argue no, she wasn't. She didn't have a choice. But, what we see is how quickly this game can play you. Scores rise and fall for arbitrary reasons, not as a reflection of a person's value. But they do become the difference between being stuck in a situation and moving forward. Something many of us have experienced.

It was only when she got off the system—or rather thrown off it—that she truly is free to speak her mind. And the ending of the episode shows just how freeing that was for her. But as anyone who traverses social media knows, saying what you want comes at a cost. Just like the old saying goes, you may have freedom of speech, but watch what you say. You can find yourself getting dragged, de-friended, blocked, ostracized, or even jailed. Community standards, somehow arbitrarily decided by the company in charge of whatever platform you're on, are brought against you for coloring outside of the lines.

Who says that authoritarianism or totalitarianism is the best way to keep a population under control? It's entirely possible that a society could emerge, where soft power keeps people in check as they dare not risk being ostracized. Good vibes only, or toxic positivity, is a way of suppressing more critical viewpoints—ones that dare to probe the origins of social problems.

If you want to see what I mean, try to critique a beloved public figure online and see the level of backlash you get. In this era of cancel culture and de-platforming, our society doles out a modern concoction of hemlock. While not as barbaric as ancient times, those in power have the means to ostracize the modern gadfly who gets too far out of line. "Nosedive" shows you what it could mean to be "canceled" in the future.

In a sense, the people that Lacie does not envy are the freest people. The truck driver she hitchhikes with is a perfect example. She said what she wanted, how she wanted, and without any mask. She wasn't phony and established clear boundaries about who she was and what she expected. When Lacie asked her if she wanted to hear her speech, she just said no, without fear of any digital consequences. She lived that life once, and realized that it only left her feeling empty. A lesson a lot of us could afford to take to heart.

After You've Watched

So here we are, at the end of the book. By now, you've watched all five seasons of *Black Mirror* and have been inspired, disturbed, amused, saddened and horrified. Maybe all in the same episode. You've seen the future and it is unnerving. You've plotted how you would escape from killer robot bees, put duct tape over your laptop's camera, and thought to yourself "maybe I shouldn't post this status update, detailing what I really think about the mayor." Those are all smart, individual measures to take. But in the grand scheme of things, it matters not—technology is barreling down on us, ready or not.

You might have seen the news of Elon Musk's latest endeavor, Neuralink. Neuralink is a brain computer interface and had a demo showcased on pigs back in August 2020. The device reads signals from the brain of the pig and can also track its limbs. Fascinating on the level of cutting edge neuroscience, but doesn't it sound a bit familiar? The fact that this tech was prototyped on a pig, and the first episode of *Black Mirror*... ahem... involves a pig, is too hilarious to leave unmentioned. Also, the tech reminds us all of the kind we saw back in "Black Museum," "The Entire History of You," and "Crocodile".

To the casual observer, there's no difference between season to season. It's all the same existential horror time after time. But, when you really stand back and look at it, *Black Mirror* has three major turning points. When it first originated, the first two seasons stayed true to form and you really knew what to expect. Then, when Netflix purchased the show it expanded the size of each season to six episodes—up from three. There was still a delicate balancing act, in that Season 3 and 4 broadened the audience, but stuck to what made *Black Mirror* what it was.

But things changed when "Bandersnatch" came out, and we would see the show take an entirely different direction. Innovative, trippy, and original, "Bandersnatch" was *Black Mirror*'s concept project, giving us an interactive episode. The effort put into giving the burgeoning fanbase something different is admirable, and it had the fanbase eager for more.

Unfortunately, then came Season 5. Instead of pulling from a pool of emerging talent like it always had, Season 5 fell into the formula of casting well-known stars, relying on that as a draw instead of a strong story. It is, for lack of a better descriptor, the most "American" season of a British show.

Season 5 of *Black Mirror* was... disappointing for a few reasons. For one, the *Black Mirror: Bandersnatch* movie was a hard act to follow. Secondly, there were less episodes, and less material to grasp with. To go back to just three episodes, from the six in Seasons 3 and 4 was jarring. Maybe there just wasn't enough material there for three more episodes?

Looking at the effort put into *Black Mirror: Bandersnatch*, it's understandable that Season 5 had only three episodes. Creator Charlie Brooker said that creating the interactive movie was so involved, that it was similar to making four or five full episodes. To really understand what happened here, we have to look at a few factors. Brooker stated in a few interviews between seasons 4 and 5, that the show would go in a decidedly less dark direction. As a result of this, the stories are not as cutting edge, impactful, or as disturbing as previous seasons.

Therein lies the struggle of a show that started with a cult following and expanded to a larger viewership—you have to keep your old fans. Not only that, but you also have to not weird out the new comers to the series too much. With star power, Season 5 definitely grew the audience, but no new ground was broken.

Brooker toned it all down a bit and people didn't like that. *Black Mirror*, in my opinion, should go back to being gritty and disturbing—especially contending with the new *Twilight Zone* out. To quote Colin from *Black Mirror: Bandersnatch* "sorry mate, wrong path."

Even after 5 seasons though, this show continues to hold our interests. And in spite of becoming more popular, it hasn't totally lost its edge yet. As a long time science fiction fan, I often compare the show to *The Twilight Zone, Outer Limits*, and even in some respects to the short lived SyFy series *Welcome to Paradox*.

This moment that we find ourselves in politically is difficult for so many people and brings some to seek escapist outlets. I've expressed the outlook that fiction in recent years has gotten more interesting, and in an odd way is an apology of sorts for the era we now find ourselves in. And that's something I believe is ripe for exploration.

Black Mirror hones in on the emptiness of our connections in this modern world. With all of these isolating technologies, people struggle to connect. It says something when people have more expansive options in the digital realm than they do in real life. Travel bans and financially restricted travel for most, but a plethora of escapist options online.

At least, that's the western world until we collectively decide differently.

However, our modern obsession with technology will not be our undoing, but only be the way it is chronicled. With humanity now in the third decade of the 21st Century, we have multiple ways to catalogue things by the second, minute, hour and day. We're creating interactive timelines and finding out that our data is not our own. Even more, we are discovering that the algorithm on most social media sites can be manipulated for commercial or political purposes.

We can thank the Cambridge Analytica scandal back in 2018 for that one. To sum it up succinctly, Cambridge Analytica harvested millions of people's data on Facebook for the purpose of selling that data to political campaigns. Fifty million users had their data harvested, and none of us knew a thing about it until a whistleblower came forward. So there we have it, folks. Our news is compromised and the social media that we participate in is vulnerable to manipulation. That's our reality.

The tragically funny thing about it though, is that we shrug it off like it's not a big deal. It's only when a show dramatizes it that we stop and think about the implications. Think about the episode "Smithereens" and how easily law enforcement worked with the social media company to track down details of Chris' life. We didn't know who got shot at the end, but just like everything else we do that involves online, we're already onto the next bit of news without having digested it fully, or grasped any significance.

In two to three weeks, whatever is trending will be forgotten, gone down the memory hole. These digitally encouraged short memories actually serve the people in power. With so many vector points of distraction, the need to focus on any one course of action is lost on thousands. Not necessarily done deliberately, but this is how it pans out. And when done deliberately, you can get away with anything by just doing something else to occupy the news.

The most unfortunate bit of it, is that it's hard to change anything. When you really sit back and understand that there are people who benefit from the way our society is, we get it. Unlike a broken game that at least gets a few patches every now and then, what is wrong with society doesn't get fixed. It's not a bug, it's a feature.

While this in of itself will not be the reason society collapses, it will give us a front view seat to watch how quickly it burns. Whether it's wildfires or gender reveal parties that get out of control, we are all watching the flames get bigger and bigger. The plausible dystopia that we've all been warned about is here, live and direct.

Too dramatic, huh? Well, look around. It's true, whether we want to acknowledge it or not. While people in my age range grew up with stories about a possible nightmare future, that future seemed much, much further off. Dystopia is already here, my dear reader.

Against The Grain: Is Black Mirror Anti-Technology?

The overarching theme of Black Mirror as an anthology is the potential downsides of current and emerging technologies. While *The Twilight Zone* was grounded in the realm of the fantastic, *Black Mirror* is steeped in plausibility of the future. This is a great part of the show's undeniable impact. This anthology entertains us with these possibilities, making us think about how we use the technology that is literally in our hands.

Throughout the show so far, we have been slipped cautionary tales about social media, crime and punishment, and the total disconnect between human beings. All of these stories have been character driven, yet in the minds of many, the plausible advancements have taken the front stage. In the last few years, any major technological breakthroughs have been compared to a possible Black Mirror episode waiting to happen.

This sentiment has been so loudly pronounced that it's easy to get the impression that Black Mirror is anti-technology. While it's an understandable takeaway from a more surface level analysis, upon deeper introspection it is decidedly not the case.

To understand true anti-technology sentiments, we can go back in history and look at an example known as the Luddites. The Luddites were a militant group of British textile workers in the early part of the 19th Century, named after Ned Ludd, a young apprentice who reportedly wrecked a textile machine in 1779. The ongoing Industrial Revolution at the time had refined the process of production, but it also meant that some workers would be replaced by machines. With their livelihoods threatened by textile machinery, they would go about sabotaging and destroying the machines. They were the anarchists of their time.

In spite of their efforts though, they went down in history as ineffective. Technologies were still introduced and their sabotage just winded up provoking crackdowns from the police. A movement that sprung up in 1811 had been, for all intents and purposes, crushed by 1813. In response, workers movements would become more sophisticated, seeing that it is more efficient to organize themselves against employers, than it is to destroy machinery.

Let's fast forward to our post-industrial, information age of the 21st Century where we're concerned about the potential abuses of technology. A time where we hear reports of horrendous working conditions in Amazon fulfillment centers. Disturbingly, we have also recently learned of Civvl, a company that is using a gig-based system to evict people from their homes. How Civvl works is that landlords hire people to process evictions for them—preying on people who just lost their jobs during the pandemic and pitting those who are desperate for work against them. It's an expression of war of all against all.

The issue in all of these examples though is not technology itself, but the application of it. If technology can be used to evict people, it can also be applied to properly house those who need shelter. According to a recent report on CNET, it is now possible to use a 3D printer to construct a home within 24 hours. And that's amazing.

Charlie Brooker in a 2019 interview said "I think that, actually, in most of our stories—if not all of our stories—the technology is neutral and what causes a problem in our stories is some sort of human failing, or weakness, or maliciousness, or clumsiness." The reality is that any innovations in of itself will be available to be used, or misused, to meet varying ends, whether or not we like it.

Consider, for example, how automation has led to the destruction of service sector jobs. Self check-out is already being used to supplant the need for a cashier. This is not a decision made by technology, but that of business owners who are using it as leverage against people who need to work for a living. The rationale here is to maximize profits, and that is really the focal point of the conflict. Technology can be used for good—it just depends on whose hands it's in.

Let's take a recent example that we're all experiencing as this writing. The entire world is in the midst of a pandemic, and the internet and various communication technologies is what's allowing people to stay connected and work from home. Whether its Facebook Live, Zoom, or Skype, we have ways to communicate despite necessary social distancing. Even though this pandemic has been horrible, it would have been far worse if we did not have such a myriad of options to stay in touch.

The last time a global health crisis wreaked havoc on the entire world was during the 1918 influenza outbreak. Obviously, there was no global network of instant communications 102 years ago. The internet itself is an outgrowth of the American military, whose original purpose was to maintain and continue military operations in the event of a nuclear war. It's not a small point that an instrument that was created to facilitate war is now being used to arguably save millions of lives. To just say that "tech is bad" would be to miss the big picture.

I've deliberately used the word grain here to refer to the technology where people get a microchip implanted in their heads. As we saw with tech like Google Glass never catching on, we can argue that Elon Musk and his Neurolink project might face the same backlash. Earlier this year, there was some misguided antipathy towards the rollout of 5G mobile networks, as conspiracy theorists believed they were responsible for spreading the coronavirus. Some even went so far as to burn 5G towers in an attempt to stop the technology from being introduced. There will always be discomfort when something new is introduced.

Extremities aside, the fact of the matter is this: technological progress is a reality of modern life. Yes, some of them will be misused, but most will be applied for honorable purposes. Some of these technologies will be used to restore what was taken away by birth defects, wars, accidents, or other circumstances. No, we are not at the point where Lieutenant Commander Geordi La Forge's visor from *Star Trek* is a reality, but there is a prototype for artificial vision being conceptualized. Second Sight, a machine assisted vision, was in development in 2019. These technologies, can become even more sophisticated. Even though it's conceptually weird now, it could become as normalized as hearing aids, prosthetic limbs, and pacemakers.

Future of Black Mirror?

Charlie Brooker has said that he has ceased creating new stories for the series at the moment. In a few interviews he's mentioned that there likely isn't an appetite for such disturbing stories during a global pandemic. And he may have a point there. We all feel like we're living in a *Black Mirror* episode already, so why watch it on Netflix? Either way, fans are not likely to see any new episodes for a long while. In 2021, *Black Mirror* will have been running for a decade and its impact has been undeniable. Some may think that *Black Mirror* is passé, and that it has run out of stories to tell, but they'd be wrong. There are more places this series could go, and the appetite is still there. In its absence, other shows like *Watchmen* and *Lovecraft Country* have come out and pushed the science fiction genre forward.

New Twilight Zone Is Not Better Than Black Mirror

Black Mirror as a show has definitely influenced the science fiction genre. Over the course of five seasons, it has touched on many aspects of life in the early 21st Century. It has even paved the way for a revival of the show that it is often compared to, *The Twilight Zone*.

Naturally, when director Jordan Peele debuted a rebooted *Twilight Zone*, I was thrilled. After seeing *Get Out* and *Us*, I was truly geeked about the possibilities of what a new *Twilight Zone* could do in this day and age. Without getting into a whole lot of the content of Jordan Peele's reboot, I will say that it has a bit of a way to go before it is on par with *Black Mirror*.

Don't get me wrong though, there are a few gem episodes over the course of its two seasons. Without saying it directly, or spoiling it, there is one episode from Season 2 that could have easily been a *Black Mirror* episode. The unfortunate part of it is that with 20 episodes over two seasons, the episodes are either hit or miss. And most of them missed. This is hard to write, because I really wanted to like this new iteration, but it's just lacking. Even if you pluck out the best episodes from the first two seasons, they don't really stand up well in comparison to Seasons 3 and 4 of *Black Mirror*.

Now this could change with subsequent seasons, but right now in this writer's opinion, *Black Mirror* is the better anthology series. That's even with the shortened, and disappointing Season 5. The issue with the rebooted *Twilight Zone,* is that it stands squarely in the shadow of the original, which has been somewhat of a curse on its multiple reboots. The 1985 reboot only lasted three seasons long, and the 2002 reboot just got one season. This reboot has too few moments to really stick in the minds of most fans. Of course, there is room for both shows to co-exist, but due to their content, the comparisons are inescapable.

There's much more to explore in the world of technology and how it affects our lives. There's a lot more to be explored as technology develops regularly, outpacing our capacity to deal with it. In all honesty, there's nothing as unnerving as the reality that we are all living in, and going through right now. At the very least, we can be entertained.

Dystopia is Now: This IS Season 6

It's almost impossible for me to write about a show with such strong dystopian messaging, without talking about the lived experiences of the moment we find ourselves in. Most of 2020 has gone by at this point, and it just gets weirder as it goes along. The coronavirus lockdowns, the curfews, the complete breakdown in trust of the U.S. government to respond properly—all of it feels surreal, like we've been cast in a movie that we never asked to be in.

Political dysfunction is the order of the day and the discourse just gets dumber and dumber as time goes on. People who failed science class are the loudest voices right now, propagating theories about how masks make people vulnerable. The wearing of a mask has somehow become a political statement. Either you are a brave anti-masker or a sheep that believes all the lies the government tells you. All attempts at a sensible dialog have broken down at this point and no one is listening. Everyone who believes what they believe, is doubling down and steeped in their accounts of what is actually happening. Some have even gone so far as to participate in mask burning protests—an explicit rejection of safety measures suggested by science. One of the biggest contradictions of our time is how people can reject science, yet still embrace and utilize technology.

From day to day, the Center for Disease Control can't make up its mind as to what it believes to be the cause of this spread. Meanwhile, we are all on our own, left mostly to our own devices to cope. Either we are without work and looking for all the help we can find or we are grinding about at home on our computers, looking for the slightest hint of good news. Slowly, in isolation, people are becoming more withdrawn and struggling to cope with a broken sense of community.

In a way, the virtual audience from "Fifteen Million Merits" is real now. We just saw it with WWE Smackdown, the NBA Games, and the MTV video music awards. What was cool and novel in 2011 has become common in 2020—and not for good reasons.

We sense that there's much more going wrong out there, but we can't put a name on all of it. If we're not concerned about getting sick, it's the increasing crime rates due to the desperation. Millions are out of work and there's no help coming from either of the major political parties.

A global sickness has unveiled the social sickness of our country for the entire world to see. The role that many thought the United States would play in the face of this emergency has turned on its head. Instead of being the leading country to battle against it, the United States has become the hardest hit. How ill is that?

Instead of utilizing the modern technologies we have to save lives, both parties insist on a dangerous reopening strategy. Pig headed politicians push the notion of herd immunity on a virus that has killed more than two million people globally. Wall Street demands that the schools reopen, safety of the children be damned. And the intransigence of these demands are met with shrugs. "Let's just do it and see what happens" seems to be the motto. As long as they who rule don't suffer too much, who cares what happens to the rest of us?

Scientists are shouted down while the most asinine conspiracy theories proliferate, threatening the discernible truth. This is a truly ugly moment, a moment in time which we have seen the worst in people—and seen it be rewarded. Not only have some of us rejected solutions, some have even rejected the possibility of a better tomorrow. Why not just let everything burn?

Oh, and things are burning as well. The skies of California are orange, looking like scenes from *Blade Runner 2049*. All the while, climate change deniers get a wider spread for their views, as it allows corporations off the hook. You as an individual can be shamed, that is pretty easy to do. But to get major companies to stop polluting would take political will and courage. Something that is woefully in short supply in this time and country. I don't even want to say that the inmates are running the asylum, because the incarcerated have more sense than to let things just go to hell like this. All of us can't escape to private houses, resorts and golf courses.

Populist electoral movements were snuffed out in the Spring, and national riots sprang up everywhere over the summer. Whether your sleep was disturbed by the wailing of ambulances, or a cache of military grade fireworks, you were expected to produce the next day as if you had gotten a full night's rest. There is no end in sight to this living nightmare, no one to point the blame at, and looks to be our reality for God knows how long.

One may say that these sort of assertions sound very cynical at a time like this. However, given all that has happened in a year, what is your counterargument? Things are too horrible to really sugarcoat it and we really shouldn't be in the first place. Yes, some have survived and thrived, but this has left no one untouched. No one is unscathed in all of this. It's in these moments you think to yourself that some of those science fiction problems don't really look so bad right now. When reality has caught up, and surpassed the dystopia that we see on our screens, all we can do is sigh.

But as Bing reminds us in "Fifteen Million Merits," "Hang on, if you must."

Appendix

Recommended Reading
Inside Black Mirror, by Jason Arnopp
Amusing Ourselves to Death, by Neil Postman
Reality is Broken, Jane McGonigal
Permanent Record, Edward Snowden

If you liked this show, you might like:
Altered Carbon
The Twilight Zone (Jordan Peele re-imagining)
World of Tomorrow, Don Hertzfeldt

Sources
Herman Cain and The Problems with Tweeting After Death: https://slate.com/technology/2020/08/herman-cain-death-twitter.html

Black Mirror's Bandersnatch: Why The Audience Never Had A Choice: https://screenrant.com/black-mirror-bandersnatch-audience-never-had-choice-reason/

The Bounds of Thinkable Thought: https://progressive.org/magazine/the-bounds-of-thinkable-thought-chomsky-851001/

Marc W. Polite

Federal Reserve Reveals Plans for Digital Dollar: https://www.forbes.com/sites/jasonbrett/2020/08/13/federal-reserve-reveals-research-plans-for-digital-dollar/#50f893af5946

Black Mirror Creator Says The World is Too Bleak Right Now for Season 6 to Happen: https://www.indiewire.com/2020/05/black-mirror-creator-season-6-world-bleak-1202229611/

Black Mirror 'Season Six' Ad Reminds Us That We're Basically Living in A Black Mirror Episode: https://metro.co.uk/2020/06/06/black-mirror-season-six-ad-reminds-us-basically-living-episode-12814529/

The New Season of Black Mirror is Here... and We're Living Through It: https://www.timeout.com/news/the-new-season-of-black-mirror-is-here-and-were-living-through-it-060420

Paul Baran, The link between nuclear war and the internet: https://www.wired.co.uk/article/h-bomb-and-the-internet

Computing And the Manhattan Project: https://www.atomicheritage.org/history/computing-and-manhattan-project

Cambridge Analytica and Online Manipulation: https://blogs.scientificamerican.com/observations/cambridge-analytica-and-online-manipulation/

She's A Model Citizen, But Can't Hide in China's "Social Credit" system: https://theheartysoul.com/citizen-cant-hide-in-chinas-social-credit-system/?utm_source=readmore

If Facebook Isn't Spying On Me, Why Did I Get Ads for What I just Spoke About?: https://theheartysoul.com/facebook-spying-ads/?utm_source=3ampp

'Zombie' Herman Cain Tweets That Coronavirus "Not As Deadly" As Media Says: https://www.huffpost.com/entry/herman-cain-coronavirus-not-as-deadly_n_5f4ca08fc5b64f17e13fc8b4

Elon Musk is One Step Closer to Connecting A Computer To Your Brain: https://www.vox.com/recode/2020/8/28/21404802/elon-musk-neuralink-brain-machine-interface-research

Black Mirror Wiki: https://black-mirror.fandom.com/wiki/Black_Mirror_Wiki

Robot Dogs Join US Air Force Exercise Giving Glimpse At Potential Battlefield of the Future: https://www.cnn.com/2020/09/09/us/robot-dogs-us-air-force-test-intl-hnk-scli-scn/index.html?utm_source=fbCNN&utm_content=2020-09-09T08%3A30%3 A06&utm_medium=social &utm_term=link

A Robot Wrote This Entire Article. Are you scared yet, human?: https://www.theguardian.com/ commentisfree /2020/sep/08/robot-wrote-this-article-gpt-3

The Online Disinhibition Effect:http://www-usr.rider.edu/~suler/psycyber/disinhibit.html

Sad Study Shows Most of Your Friends Don't Actually Like You: https://www.complex.com/life/2016/05/study-friends-dont-like-you

List of Fictional Games from TuckerSoft: https://www.tuckersoft.net/ealing20541/history/

U.S. Lawmakers Concerned by Accuracy of Facial Recognition: https://www.bbc.com/news/technology-51130904

Startup Recruits Cash Strapped Gig Workers To Help Landlords Evict Tenants: https://nypost.com/2020/09/22/startup-civvl-recruits-cash-strapped-gig-workers-to-help-landlords-evict-tenants/?utm_source=email_site buttons&utm_medium=site%20buttons&utm_campaign=site%20buttons

What is the Memory Capacity of the Human Brain?: https://www.scientificamerican.com/article/what-is-the-memory-capacity/

Black Mirror Producers Says Technology Isn't The Enemy: https://www.syfy.com/syfywire/watch-black-mirror-producers-say-technology-isnt-the-enemy

Houses 3D Printed in Just 24 Hours Now Shipping in California: https://www.cnet.com/news/houses-3d-printed-in-just-24-hours-now-shipping-in-california/

About The Author

Marc W. Polite is a writer, author, blogger, and poet from New York City (born and raised) who cannot stop talking about science fiction. He has been a fan of the genre since he was a child. Whether it was *Star Wars, Star Trek, War of the World*s, or *Lost in Space*, he watched it all. He has always been fascinated by depictions of the future, and contrasting the emerging technology with what it means to be truly human.

He has been a die-hard science fiction fan from the time he was in elementary school. Growing up, I was heavy into *Tales from The Crypt, Beyond Tomorrow* and *Alien Nation* among many other shows of the era. Being fascinated with far off worlds, and a possible different future, he took to these stories of far off reality.

As an introverted adolescent, the real world was a place of constant threats. He used to keep up with *Starlog* magazine, *Electronic Gaming Monthly*, and watch shows like the classic *V*. Growing up in Harlem, he was a sci-fi head and a gamer before it was cool. In the 90's, he hopped around from arcade to arcade, sonning everyone he could in both Street Fighter and Mortal Kombat. Ask about me.

He is the author of three books: *The Poetic Ruminations of Mr. Born Nice*, *Everything To Learn,*

Marc W. Polite

Nothing To Teach, and *Poetic Ruminations Volume 2*. He has also contributed to the anthology *1984 in the 21st Century*. Currently, he is a proud member of the legendary Harlem Writers Guild, and can be found sharing silly cat memes on Instagram when not penning poems or vociferous op eds.

Other Riverdale Avenue Books You Might Like

The Binge Watcher's Guide to Doctor Who:
A History of the Doctor Who
and the First Female Doctor
By Mackenzie Flohr

The Binge Watcher's Guide to the
Films of Harry Potter
An Unauthorized Guide
By Cecilia Tan

The Binge Watcher's Guide to
The Handmaid's Tale
An Unofficial Companion
By Jamie K. Schmidt

1984 in the 21st Century:
An Anthology of Essays
Edited by Lori Perkins'

Everything You Always Wanted
to Know about Watergate*
*But Were Afraid to Ask
By Brian O'Connor and Lori Perkins

If you liked this book,
Please join our mailing list at riverdaleavebooks.com

www.ingramcontent.com/pod-product-compliance
Lightning Source LLC
Chambersburg PA
CBHW050107170426
43198CB00014B/2497